Capricorn

1995

TERI KING'S
ASTROLOGICAL HOROSCOPES
FOR 1995

Capricorn

Teri King's complete horoscope
for all those whose birthdays
fall between
22 December and 20 January

E L E M E N T
Shaftesbury, Dorset ● Rockport, Massachusetts
Brisbane, Queensland

© Teri King 1994

Published in Great Britain in 1994 by
Element Books Limited
Longmead, Shaftesbury, Dorset

Published in the USA in 1994 by
Element, Inc
42 Broadway, Rockport, MA 01966

Published in Australia in 1994 by
Element Books Limited for
Jacaranda Wiley Limited
33 Park Road, Milton, Brisbane, 4064

Cover design by Max Fairbrother
Text design by Roger Lightfoot
Typeset by The Electronic Book Factory Ltd, Fife
Printed and bound in Great Britain by
BPC Paperbacks Ltd, Aylesbury, Bucks

British Library Cataloguing in Publication
data available

Library of Congress Cataloging in Publication
data available

ISBN 1–85230–515–0

Element Books regrets that it cannot enter into any
correspondence with readers requesting information
about their horoscope.

Contents

Contents

Introduction

Astrology has many uses, not least of these its ability to help us to understand both ourselves and other people. Unfortunately there are many misconceptions and confusions associated with it, such as that old chestnut – how can the zodiac forecast be accurate for all the millions of people born under one particular sign?

The answer to this is that all horoscopes published in newspapers, books and magazines are, of necessity, of a general nature. Unless an astrologer can work from the date, time and place of your birth, the reading given will only be true for the typical member of your sign.

For instance, let's take a person born on 9 August. This person is principally a subject of Leo, simply because the Sun occupied that section of the heavens known as Leo during 24 July to 23 August. However, when delving into astrology at its most serious, there are other influences which need to be taken into consideration. For example, the Moon. This planet enters a fresh sign every 48 hours. On the birth date in question it may have been in, say, Virgo. And if this were the case it would make our particular subject Leo (Sun representing willpower) and Virgo (Moon representing instincts) or if you will a Leo/Virgo. Then again the rising sign or 'ascendant' must also be taken into consideration. This also changes constantly as the earth revolves: approximately every two hours a new section of the heavens comes into view – a new sign passes over the horizon. The rising sign is of the utmost importance, determining the image projected by the subject to the outside world – in effect, the personality.

The time of birth is essential when compiling a birth chart. Let us suppose that in this particular instance Leo was rising at the time of birth. Now, because two of the three main influences are Leo, our sample case would be fairly typical of his/her sign, possessing all the faults and attributes associated with it. However, if on the other hand, the Moon and ascendant had been in Virgo then, whilst our subject would certainly display some of the Leo attributes or faults, it is more than likely that for the most part he/she would feel and behave more like a Virgoan.

As if life weren't complicated enough, this procedure must be carried through to take into account all the remaining planets. The position and signs of Mercury, Venus, Mars, Jupiter, Saturn, Uranus, Neptune and Pluto must all be discovered, plus the aspect formed from one planet to another. The calculation and interpretation of these movements by an astrologer will then produce an individual birth chart.

Because the heavens are constantly changing, people with identical charts are a very rare occurrence. Although it is not inconceivable that it could happen, this would mean that the two subjects were born not only on the same date and at the same time, but also in the same place. Should such an incident occur, then the deciding factors as to how these individuals would differ in their approach to life, love, career, financial prospects and so on would be due to environmental and parental influence.

Returning to our hypothetical Leo: our example with the rising Sun in Leo and Moon in Virgo, may find it useful not only to read up on his or her Sun sign (Leo) but also to read the section dealing with Virgo (the Moon). Nevertheless, this does not invalidate Sun sign astrology. This is because of the great power the Sun possesses, and on any chart this planet plays an important role.

Belief in astrology does not necessarily mean believing in totally determined lives, that we are predestined and have no control over our fate. But what it does clearly show is that our lives run in cycles, for both good and bad and, with the aid of astrology, we can make the most of, or minimize, certain patterns and tendencies. How this is done is entirely up to the individual. For example, if you are in possession of the knowledge that you are about to experience a lucky few days or weeks, then you can make the most of them by pushing ahead with plans. You can also be better prepared for illness, misfortune, romantic upset and every adversity.

Astrology should be used as it was originally intended – as a guide, especially to character. In this direction it is invaluable and it can help us in all aspects of friendship, work and romance. It makes it easier for us to see ourselves as we really are and, what's more, as others see us. We can recognize both our own weaknesses and strengths and those of others. It can give us both outer confidence, and inner peace.

In the following pages you will find: personality profiles; an in-depth look at the year ahead from all possible angles including numerology; monthly and daily guides; plus, and it is a big plus, information for those poor and confused creatures so often ignored who are born on 'the cusp' – at the beginning or the end of each sign.

Used wisely, astrology can help you through life. It is not intended to encourage complacency, since in the final analysis what you do with your life is up to you. This book will aid you in adopting the correct attitude to the year ahead and thus maximizing your chances of success. Positive thinking is encouraged because this helps us to attract positive situations. Allow astrology to walk hand in hand with you and you will be increasing your chances of success and happiness.

A Fresh Look at Your Sun Sign

As a rule, members of the general public appreciate and understand that for practical reasons Sun sign astrology is fairly general, and therefore for a more in-depth study it is necessary to hire an astrologer who will then proceed to study the date, year, place and time of birth of an individual. Then, by correlating the birth chart with the positions of the different planets, a picture can be slowly drawn for the client.

However, there is also a middle way, which can be illuminating. Each sign comprises 30 'degrees' (or days) and, by reducing these down into three sections, it becomes possible to draw up a picture of each sign which is far more intimate than the usual methods. Therefore, check out your date of birth and draw your own conclusions from the information below.

CAPRICORN (22 December to 20 January)

BORN BETWEEN 22 DECEMBER AND 1 JANUARY

Your Sun falls in the first section of Capricorn, making you ambitious, often solemn, successful and somewhat detached on occasions. You are also disciplined, hardworking and prone to depressive moods.

The ideas and opinions of other people tend to be of great importance to you. This is because you are basically insecure in yourself. Therefore you are inclined to socialize with those whom you respect since you see yourself reflected in your relationships. It is very much a case of 'who you know and not what you know' that counts with you.

You are inclined to be status conscious and critical, and you prefer that people don't take up your time unnecessarily. At the same time, you are dutiful, devoted and often loyal towards those people to whom you are deeply committed.

Because you have plenty of common sense and practical ability, plus an earthy personality, you have little time and patience with the flighty members of the human race who never seem to know whether they are coming or going. For the most part, you are drawn to people with qualities of strength, honesty, stability and intelligence and who have accomplished a great deal in this world. In other words, you have the highest personal ideals.

When it comes to your personal life, and especially where love is concerned, you are drawn to those who are in prominent positions. However, due to your deep-seated insecurities, you frequently become involved with people beneath your own level of accomplishment as they tend to make you look good in the eyes of the world.

Because your own drive for status is so important, you ultimately dismiss from your life and your social circle those who you feel are in a position to bring you down. It is very likely that by the middle of your life you will have proved your own worth and are likely to have found success in a highly competitive society.

BORN BETWEEN 2 JANUARY AND 11 JANUARY

Your Sun falls in the second section of Capricorn, giving you a tremendous amount of charm and sociability. It is likely that you are gifted in a creative way. In business you are very shrewd where financial matters are concerned, and in your social life you show a gracious and unmistakeable flair.

It is likely that you are a highly productive person who is driven to work a great deal and sleep very little. You are tactful, understanding, sincere, kind, adaptable and diplomatic. You possess a highly individualistic and unique value system which helps you when it comes to determining your life objectives. You climb towards these objectives with a bravery and a tenacity that are never deflected.

Capricorns born in this section have an overwhelming need to make concrete their desires, despite the strength of any opposition they are confronted with, and they do it with such dogged determination that others, including rivals, look on with fascination.

Subjects of this section often show an inclination to subdue the pleasure principle should a situation of long-term profit be at stake. Furthermore they feel a sense of great dedication to professional duties and ideals as well as exhibiting a conscientious approach towards details.

On the romantic side, early in your life there is likely to have been some disappointment and heartache from a destroyed marriage or relationship. However, if you can fight an inclination to become embittered or disillusioned about this, then it is likely that this unfortunate experience will be followed by an extremely happy union with a devoted, loyal mate.

Capricorns born in this section possess a powerful and determined will. The moment you come to trust and rely on it is the time when your potential will become limitless.

BORN BETWEEN 12 JANUARY AND 20 JANUARY

Your Sun falls in the third section of Capricorn. Because of this, you are a Utopian whose ideals tend to become caught between logic and emotions. This frequently causes you to suffer extreme anxiety when confronted with choices that will significantly affect your life. You are inclined to brood about past mistakes and decisions and often bring on your own states of depression.

Certainly your mind can be highly disciplined when you refuse to allow it to control you through negative mood swings and depressions. You are an intellectual person with a steady nature and a strong sense of purpose and destiny.

Although you can become bogged down with details of an administrative nature, you frequently have your own interests, often in the sort of creative activities that could be put to professional use. However, first you must confront your own fears and phobias because they can severely restrict your potential for growth and expansion.

Because you are modest and shy, you often have problems, either of making yourself heard or of communicating on a deep level. Although your ideas can be viable and strong, your means of expressing them tend to be incoherent or weak, as a result of which you often suffer from a lack of publicity.

There is a latent writing ability and verbal talent in this section. However, first you must be able to trust yourself and believe that you are a powerful person. The world may very well be waiting for your talents and ideas. Consider the notion that you might be doing everyone around you a favour by pushing yourself into the limelight. Be more prepared to participate in the world around you. In this way you will be making the most of your potential.

WHEN YOU ARE BAD YOU ARE VERY VERY BAD (Horrorscopes)

There is a tendency for you to be condescending towards others due to a complex which compels you to try to control people. You tend to be shackled to your own will and you suffer nagging discontent if you do not feel free to enact your power play.

Because of your great ego problems, you experience a need always to be on top. One of your favourite experiences is ordering other people around and telling them what to do as if they were incompetents who cannot function without the 'pearls of wisdom' you subject them to.

You are patronizing, domineering and arrogant, and you tend to override the feelings of others to such a degree that you treat them as if they were pieces of furniture. You are inclined to judge other people by their success and to ingratiate yourself with them. You have precious little time or patience for those who are beneath you, and you deliberately cultivate the more successful members of the human race. Because of your self-obsession, you live each day in the hope that it will bring you closer to being able to exercise your power games.

Other people might call you stuffy, others again a sour puss; this is because of your obvious self-importance and your surprising way of taking others down and trampling on their egos. Your motivating principle drives you to prove your superiority, and you need to demonstrate other people's inferiority.

Your personality is so infuriating that it could bring a saint to contemplate homocide. After a while of listening to you, others will do anything to keep you quiet. You are inclined to boast in an effort to convince the world that you are something that you really are not.

When it comes to love, you have a way of making the opposite sex feel as if you have just rescued them from a fate worse than death. One of the most interesting and complicated things about you is that when you have made up your mind that a certain person is your soulmate, then you proceed to disregard totally their thoughts and opinions.

Your fundamental attitude to your partner is that he or she was meant to live to serve you and should be sensitive enough to know when to keep quiet and listen to what you have to say. Their thoughts and opinions are completely ignored, since you believe that you always know best.

Because a mate is as necessary to you as a pair of shoes or a nice warm bed, it is important to ensure that you get the type that looks good but costs least. If after a certain amount of time has elapsed it begins to dawn on you that the person concerned just isn't interested, then you become morose, hostile and defensive. For in your mind it is only *your* feelings that matter, since he or she simply isn't allowed the right to have any opinions themselves. Despite this, you never give up and proceed to apply pressure until your victim's resistance fades away and they are left grovelling for peace. However, you are oblivious to their plight. To you, all that is important is power, the kind that will put you at the top where you can rule your kingdom with an iron fist.

CUSP CASES

CAPRICORN/SAGITTARIUS CUSP:
19-24 DECEMBER

When the heat of the furnace of Sagittarius is combined with the powerful dynamics associated with the earthy Capricorn, great leadership, achievement and success are all possible. This combination makes you both generous, traditional, freedom-loving and restrained. Furthermore you are cautious, independent and inclined to produce a slight conflict between your inner and outer personality and needs.

Your natural friendliness is blended with good judgement and foresight, therefore you are the sort of person who can usually make your fantasies come true. You make a formidable partner or adversary and one who has the power to excel both creatively and romantically, yet at the same time give solid support to those who count.

CAPRICORN/AQUARIUS CUSP: 18-23 JANUARY

You are an inventive and eccentric genius with a large streak of common sense. Invariably you have your eye firmly fixed on the future, although you are also ready to learn from the past. With your leadership and organizational ability, plus your humanitarian ideals, you could make a successful and highly popular politician.

Your Capricorn side could hold back your Aquarian inclination to race ahead without due thought, and it will have the patience to see you through the tough times in life.

You love working with other people for their own benefit, something which is generally much appreciated by your mate. You are witty and articulate with a talent to amuse, a trait which is certainly appreciated and admired by the opposite sex.

The Year Ahead: Overview

It is no easy matter being born under the sign of the goat for no one is quite as emotionally cut-off or isolated as you are from your fellow creatures.

It is all but impossible for you to communicate the depths of your feelings in the usual ways, and it is your approach to life which is often your problem. This is because you appear to be a little too stiff with others, cautious and sometimes even brusque. It is not your fault really, rather a peculiarity of your sign. You can't help but erect a thick wall around yourself in order to protect that acute sensitivity. Actually you are brave, fearless and strong in a worldly way, but you are secretly terrified of being hurt emotionally. Others seldom realize that beneath that superb self-control lies a gentle, soft and vulnerable, but anxious, person. What makes it even more difficult is the fact that you are only too aware of your inner sensitivity. It is hardly surprising then that your approach to the new year tends to be ambivalent. One moment you are possibly filled with anticipation and eagerness, and the next feelings of dread slowly begin to overwhelm you.

Now, let's take a look and see whether those fears of yours are justified, and if not, help you to dispel them and look towards the future in a more positive and courageous fashion. It might help you to understand that each year of your life should be viewed as a challenge, a chance to shine and an opportunity for you to expand and grow.

During 1995, certain lessons are laid before you and it is up to you whether or not you pick up the gauntlet and bravely push out into life. Certainly you possess the courage to do so. From January until August it seems that you have learned how to establish yourself on a wider basis by constructively using your emotional talents in some form of individual creative self-expression, perhaps through having children, or through hobbies or the pursuit of pleasure in general. Once these lessons have been learned, you should be turning your attention to stabilizing your position in the world and attempting to realize your secret hopes and wishes. Should you decide to follow this path, you will find that your friends, acquaintances and contacts will help you to realize your own talents and directly or indirectly help you to determine your standing in the world.

From August onwards, there is a suggestion that you will have come to terms with your immediate environment and will have sought to identify yourself with one chosen part of it in a more specialized way. You have learned to deal with matters related to your parents, your family life, your past experiences and everything which has given you a feeling of security. You now know how to use your experience in order to further your ambitions and should be pushing out into life. Now it is time to project yourself on to your community, and to use your talents to fulfil your professional aims. You will receive help and guidance from an older relative, perhaps a parent. Push ahead with your professional desires with your usual grit and determination and you will be able to accomplish a great deal during this year.

Both Neptune and Uranus have been in your sign

now for many years, causing you to feel confused, muddled and uncertain about the future, and prone to unexpected setbacks, disappointments and complications. Now you can begin to feel more optimistic. Whilst Neptune continues in your sign for the entire year, it will only affect those of you born during the last five days of the Capricorn period. Should this apply to you, then you should use the positive influences of Neptune, a planet which represents a certain amount of muddle but which can also fill you with inspiration on occasions as well as idealism. Try to use these gifts constructively in order to help you through the year ahead.

Uranus is struggling to free itself from your sign and actually manages to do so for a short while between April and early June. During these two months, stresses and strains, as well as struggles of recent years, will begin to fade away and you will adopt a much more relaxed attitude towards life. However, even though Uranus will be occupying your sign during the earlier and latter parts of this year, nevertheless, it will only affect you if you were born during the last two days of the Capricorn period. Therefore in the main, most of you will be free from the chaos and unexpected setbacks you have been prone to for the last four years.

Despite this, it is always wise to remember that each planet has both its positive and negative influences. In the case of Uranus, the unexpected can be exciting and challenging, providing you are prepared to become more adaptable and alter your plans and ambitions accordingly. However, those of you who stubbornly refuse to alter course regardless of circumstances will make life difficult for yourselves. Of course, you tend to pursue an ambition or objective relentlessly, regardless of opposition, when perhaps you should stop, consider and accept the new circumstances which have arisen and adjust your plans accordingly. Therefore if you have experienced the feeling of ramming your head against a brick wall over the last couple of years, this has been due to your inability to adapt. It is important for you to learn then that nothing ever stays the same. And instead of fearing the new, you should be ready to embrace it with open arms.

Pluto too is valiantly pushing its way through Scorpio and into the following sign of Sagittarius. It temporarily enters this sign between January and March, and is finally successful during November.

Whilst Pluto has been wending its way through Scorpio and continues to do so on and off throughout the year, no doubt you have been experiencing many frustrations, sudden beginnings and endings in your friendship circle and also in your objectives in life. Once more, the more adaptable you can be to fresh sets of circumstances which crop up, the easier your life can be. And to this end it is important that you read the month-to-month guides which will help you to adopt the correct attitude at any given time during the year.

Throughout the year ahead, Saturn will be in the sign of Pisces and because of this you must ensure that your mind is careful but not narrow, exacting without being slow, conscientious whilst avoiding over-conscientiousness, serious but not melancholic, persevering but not laborious, and concentrated and reflective without giving in to morbid thoughts. Last year you may have discovered whilst travelling from place to place that life can be unduly complicated by delays. However, should you be sensible enough to allow more time when travelling, then you will avoid any unnecessary difficulties.

For the entire year, Jupiter will be situated in the sign of Sagittarius. This will increase your faith in providence, encourage philanthropic deeds, and supply you with the necessary willpower and determination to win over opposition and even enemies. This is a particularly lucky placing for those of you who work in the medical profession or in any situation which needs a great deal of contemplation or intuition. Remember that although you possess a sensible head on your shoulders, there are times when you are unaware of your gut feelings and when you fail to listen to them, too often you live to regret it. Jupiter will be providing you with opportunities to secure the fulfilment of your hopes and wishes on many levels and in many directions. It will also be helping you to become more integrated with your life and those around you. Given your wonderful determination, it will help you to turn pipe dreams into reality as well as eliminating frustration and antisocial behaviour.

On a more universal level, once Pluto finally struggles free of the clutches of Scorpio into Sagittarius, we shall all have a great deal more to look forward to. During the ensuing years, man will have left his uncomfortable 'teen years' behind and will be behaving in a more responsible manner. Instead of making token gestures towards clearing up the pollution on mother earth, giant strides will be made. Black will find it easier to live with White, man will cease to fight woman, Jew will cease to hate Muslim. The leaders of our nations will slowly realize that they must be less self-seeking and will be more concerned with the people who have elected them or over whom they rule. Medical breakthroughs will banish many illnesses and diseases which currently plague us and our life expectancy and quality of life will be increased in realistic terms. It is also likely that we may finally realize that while modern technology can be a tremendous help to man it can also be destructive. At the time of writing, many of us have been denied the opportunity to work and build a life for ourselves. Soon it will be realized that this state of affairs simply cannot be allowed to continue. True, this realization may not be reached until individual countries simply can no longer afford to keep billions of their population dependent on the state, and understand that unless something is done to stop the progress of technology then we will be bringing about our own destruction.

Man must be free to create, work and keep his dignity. And if Pluto in Sagittarius cannot reawaken man's consciousness then nothing can. Clearly then, we all have a good deal to look forward to, and in your case, Capricorn, it is important to remain hopeful and optimistic about the future.

In order that you may make the most out of 1995, refer to the monthly guides which will help you to stay buoyant and stable, and extract the maximum out of the year ahead.

Career Year

When it comes to work, you need security and regular pay above all else to give you peace of mind. This should be kept in mind when choosing a job. Any effort to get rich quick would normally not appeal and should be discouraged. You should aim for steady progress on a long-term basis as for you the sky can be the limit. By hook or by crook, you will reach the top of your profession. Certainly you enjoy fame and publicity. Your career can be so important to you that all else is excluded. At some point during your life you will more than likely be attracted to the ruthless field of politics, but sudden disillusionment could make this a brief experience.

Any position where patience, economic ability and emotional detachment can be exercised and developed will be suitable. You need somewhere you can establish authority and devise constructive systems of production and administration for the benefit of the community or a business.

You could do well as a scientist, head teacher, manager, engineer, civil servant, mathematician, farmer, politician, builder, osteopath, surveyor, architect, dentist or musician (this sign often possesses musical ability).

But what of your professional luck during 1995? Because of the position of Neptune in your sign, you could gain in any job which allows you to be a visionary and to be idealistic, receptive, imaginative, artistic, publicity seeking and even whimsical.

During the months when Uranus is in your sign (see monthly guides), you will be drawn to opportunities for being independent (such as freelance work), original, unconventional and possibly scientific.

Because the feeling of change continues on and off throughout this year, it is essential that you become more compliant and receptive to ideas and developments which may occur completely out of the blue. Failure to do so could lead to a certain amount of stress.

Pluto's position in Scorpio for the majority of the year will certainly aid those of you who depend on friendship and contacts to make a living. It will be a productive time too for the reformers and idealists among you, such as politicians. You will find it a good deal easier to influence your friends, contacts and acquaintances.

Saturn in Pisces will aid those of you who work in jobs where an exact and careful approach is needed. You are likely to be more than usually conscientious and serious where your work is concerned, particularly if you work in the media, in sales or in buying. Concentration is enhanced too and this will certainly be useful for those of you who work on anything which could be described as intricate.

However, should your job necessitate a great deal of travelling, then you must take extra care to be punctual as delays affecting all kinds of transport could create an unfortunate impression on bosses or potential clients.

This is certainly likely to be a fruitful and successful year for those of you who are at all creative. Saturn will be providing you with the ability to give ideas constructive shape and form, and because you are more impressionable than usual, you will be able to respond to environments and situations and use them in your work.

Jupiter's journey through Sagittarius for the entire year will be boosting your inner confidence and aiding you when it comes to triumphing over opposition or enemies. Should your work be of a contemplative nature or behind the scenes such as in the medical profession, in research, or maybe through an invention, then you can expect a profitable and productive time.

Should you be unfortunate enough to be unemployed, then renew your optimism and your faith in the future. Use the monthly guides and you should be able to remedy this situation.

Those of you who secretly yearn to form your own company or firm should use 1995 for laying down the foundations to make this dream come true. This is an ideal year for slowly gathering the information and facts that you need so that you will be ready to blossom and strike out on your own during 1996. Throughout this year, try to remember that Jupiter will be entering your sign during 1996 and you must be ready to plunge into life and make all those hopes and wishes of yours come true. It can be done, providing you retain a positive frame of mind and belief in yourself and talents.

Should your work be of the kind that relies on contacts, you will find that late October through to the middle part of November is the time when others are most likely to be open to your ideas and suggestions. Professional partnerships can be formed successfully during the month of July.

There is little to hold you back during this year, Capricorn. It is only self-imposed restrictions which you need to fight. Remember that the world is out there, waiting for your talents and your skills. All you need is the confidence and belief in yourself which will enable you to make 1995 a memorable time. Bear in mind too that the stars impel; they do not compel. It is up to you to take control of your life and drive yourself towards the fulfilment of your dreams. However, make sure you do so at a step at a time for that is the Capricorn way. Those of you who are looking for overnight success are rarely lucky. Yours is not a sign which achieves prosperity in this way. Work steadily and conscientiously towards your goal and you can be confident of success either this year or next.

You have a lot to offer life, so maintain a belief in yourself and you simply cannot go wrong.

Money Year

Providing you are not a 'giddy goat', and some of you may well be, then you are generally shrewd about cash, so much so that you could be a financial wizard. Generally speaking, you know how to make money, keep it and help it to grow. You have the tenacity of a tycoon and the wits of a confidence trickster.

As a rule, you are certainly hard-headed, realistic and willing to work when it comes to money. It really doesn't matter how much you earn, somehow you invariably manage to put away something for the proverbial rainy day. Most of the time you are frugal, even bordering on stingy and cheap. However, from time to time a self-indulgent mood suddenly descends and then you can spend a small fortune in an hour on a shopping spree. Despite this, because you have such excellent taste, invariably your money is invested well, even though it may leave you short for quite a while. Everything you buy brings with it a great deal of pleasure for the future.

The trouble with some Capricorns is that they tend to live just to work and consider money almost of secondary importance. If this applies to you, then cash is simply a bonus for you. You would probably work extremely long hours for nothing should the opportunity arise. Basically what you are looking for is recognition and prestige.

Despite your disregard of, money, Capricorn is one

sign that is very rarely seen on the bread line. This is
because in general you are at your best when working
under pressure and difficulties only strengthen your
resolve to do well in life. A lesson for you to learn
in this area is not to become so preoccupied with
career that you forget how to enjoy life. Remember
that although it is all right to work hard, it is equally
important to play hard if you are to be a well-rounded
person. Although you are one sign who can endure
a great deal of hardship and deprivation, this is not
necessarily the way you will prefer to live. Everything
in life comes to you through persistent effort and that
includes cash. The only enemy you have is yourself, as
it is likely that you are very insecure with a tendency
to think negatively when life is against you. Luckily
you also have a tremendous amount of determination and once you are able to gather your courage
once more and start to fight then you will realize
that you are an unbeatable force. Never let anyone
or anything get you down, Capricorn, for when you
are on form, opposition melts away in the face of
your relentless pursuit of your ambitions. Once you
have recognized this, you will never allow anything
to get you down – well, not for any length of time
anyway.

How will you fare in 1995? In order to discover this we
must turn to the planet which influences your finances
which is the erratic, exciting and inspired Uranus.
Certainly this planet is capable of creating a certain
amount of surprise, shocks and even complications, but
it can also supply you with unexpected opportunities. It
is basically a question about how adaptable you can be
regarding fresh ideas and developments. Possibly of late
you have allowed this planet's unpredictable behaviour
to get you down, when you should have risen to the
bait, got out your determination and grappled with

the circumstances in order to triumph which you most certainly can do.

For most of the year, Uranus will be in your sign (for the exceptions to this, refer to the monthly guides) and because of this, adaptability and an open mind will clearly serve you well. Certainly you are not given to speculation as it is far too unreliable for your sensible practical nature, but despite this when opportunities present themselves as they definitely will, then you must be ready to throw off the old and take on board the new.

It is likely too that you could gain through unusual people and unusual sources. Don't allow your conservative nature to hold you back then. You are the type who tends to stick to familiar paths and who plans ahead far into the future. This year you will be wise to make plans for a month at a time with one eye on the future, but do not lay down hard and fast rules and insist on sticking to them no matter what. Remember that life has a way of throwing out surprises, and instead of falling by the wayside when this occurs, you must be ready to seize exciting possibilities in every way you can.

Capricorn is a sign that simply cannot resist a bargain, but with Saturn in the sign of Pisces for the entire year, it is very likely that no such thing as a bargain will exist during this particular year. Therefore, if you deliberately go out looking for one, you are likely to be fobbed off with shoddy inferior goods. Be prepared to have to pay over the odds for what you want out of life, but try not to go completely over the top.

When it comes to making financial decisions, you would be well advised to rely on your instincts instead of your busy brain. This is because the position of Jupiter on your chart will be increasing your intuition in all areas, including financial matters.

There is also likely to be a tendency for you to be

over-idealistic when negotiating, thanks to the presence of Neptune in your sign. You must try hard to ignore this and stay practical at all times. When it comes to the basics, money is about as basic as you can get and it really has very little to do with ideals. When you confuse the two you could very well be the loser.

Those of you who are struggling to survive as self-employed or freelance workers should step up your efforts. Do not be discouraged by recent setbacks, but drag out your Capricorn persistence and all of your effort will certainly pay off during 1996. This year should therefore be used as a preparation time for a more successful future. Bear this in mind and it will help you to get through those darker moods and moments.

When it comes to enjoyment or holidays, you will be strongly tempted to cut back completely. However, this is foolhardy. Remember that you work extremely hard, but you must have a certain amount of relaxation. This doesn't necessarily mean giving in to extravagant impulses. If you cannot afford a couple of weeks away at some point, do not deny yourself completely, but settle for a weekend here and a weekend there. You will discover that a break away from boring routine will help you to return to your problems renewed, refreshed and ready to do battle once more.

If, for whatever reason you have become embroiled in what seems to be an impossible situation then do not battle on alone. Seek the advice of a professional who will be able to lift the load from your shoulders and lay down a plan for the future which you must stick to.

Armed with the above advice you should be able to make this year one when you will at least break even. You should have the strong smell of success in your nostrils by December. Use the promise of rewards in 1996 as your carrot and follow your path towards success and financial enrichment with tenacity, persistence and a positive attitude.

Remember that negative thinking can frequently bring about that which we most fear. This will help you to overcome yourself and in that way you will have learned the greatest lesson you will probably ever have to learn in life.

The nicest thing about the year ahead is that you are likely to be freer to follow your own path and more positive that you are on the right track. This is clearly backed up by the stars.

Love and Sex Year

As a rule, you can hardly be described as a raving sex maniac for you usually pour most of your energies into your career. One reason for this is a need for security. You do not wait for someone else to supply your basic needs, but prefer to rely on yourself. Because of tiredness or pressure of work it may not be easy for you to relax and achieve orgasm. Ideally you need a partner who can introduce a light-hearted influence into your life as sex is frequently taken far too seriously. You should try to understand that it can be fun, even hilarious on occasions.

When unable to achieve orgasm, there is no need for you to feel like a failure; this is the worst thing you could possibly do. The odd occasional problem should be dismissed unless it becomes a regular occurrence. Even then, you should try to remember that it does take two to achieve this happy state in most cases. Although you do not feel that complicated sexual positions are particularly stimulating, they can certainly be amusing. Because of this, they could help to bring laughter and relaxation into your sex life.

Often the best aphrodisiac for you, and certainly this is true this year, is to laugh your way into bed, the objective being to break down tension. Massage will also work miracles for you, especially when done with oil. A true Capricorn may be a proficient lover but rarely goes in for anything too ambitious or unusual for you are conservative at heart. Therefore, if your partner suggests anything outrageous, make sure it is done in an amusing way.

Very often your idea of being outrageous is having a bit of fun on the side whilst going about your professional duties. What you need is a partner who can show you that you 'ain't seen nothing yet'. After all, why should you settle for second best when you have an expert at home?

During this particular year, the continuing presence of Neptune in your sign is likely to be encouraging the romantic side of your nature. There will be times, of course, when there are exceptions to the rule; to find out more about this, refer to the monthly guides. However, in the main, if you are single you will be out there looking for that special someone. Now, Capricorn, have you not learned yet that when we look we do not always find? Try to relax a little bit more and you may find Mr or Miss Right walking into your life. Although you are highly organized, this is one side of life which you cannot control. Emotions have a way of taking flight when we least expect them and this is certainly going to be the pattern during this particular year.

If you are single, then the best time for meeting that special someone is during February and again in July. In the main, though, it seems that you are too preoccupied with other sides of life to consider settling down.

If you are already in a relationship, then do not allow other considerations such as work or money to interfere with your personal life. Strive hard to balance your life so that you not only work hard but also play hard. Remember that with the right person in your life you can be spurred on to greater achievements at work, and certainly those ambitions are foremost to your character if you are a typical Capricorn.

On a purely sexual level, December looks to be the

month when you will be most tempted to stray if you are in a relationship. If you are single, this will be a time when you will be at your most promiscuous and must take the necessary precautions to safeguard your precious health.

This can certainly be an exciting and interesting year, providing you can keep a sense of balance. Whether you choose to or not, of course, is entirely up to you.

Health and Diet Year

SPIRITUAL WELLBEING

Many people, including myself, are rapidly beginning to recognize the fact that mental attitude can and does have a direct effect on physical wellbeing. Some would argue that 'spiritual health' also plays a large part in maintaining a healthy body as well as a healthy mind. This is not to suggest that we must strive for 'sainthood' but, nevertheless, we should be aware of being on the right path – our journey towards some objective.

It is necessary to be conscious of our beliefs and our goals otherwise it is quite likely that we may lose our way and then our physical wellbeing may be affected by a sense of futility which can undermine our health. You know the kind of attitude: 'Is it really worth putting myself out?' 'I try but it doesn't seem to get me anywhere'. Most of us can recognize these feelings at some stages in our life. Should such an attitude occur and be followed by several unfortunate setbacks, which we all must occasionally experience, then this can initially dent our confidence and even more serious problems may occur if we allow ourselves to be pulled under. Believing we are getting nowhere seems to take all the joy out of life and certainly undermines our health. Deep down within our soul, we hunger for chances for growth and, when this is denied, how can we expect to retain bodily health if we lack the life or will to go on?

Positive thinking can go a long way to keeping us hale and hearty. Perfect health encompasses the wholeness of mind, body and spirit.

HEALTH AND DIET

As a goat, you are always willing to be of practical assistance to other people. But like Cancer, your opposite sign, you tend to fret easily and suffer from stress. The most likely cause of illness for you is your tendency to bottle up your emotions. In fact, all too frequently you give the impression of being totally unemotional. Your inner sense of propriety and dignity make it difficult for you to express your feelings. If, in addition, you were brought up by parents who believed in keeping their feelings under wraps, then this will have laid the foundations for psychosomatic illnesses which later in life can result in nervous problems which may restrict movement. It is therefore of utmost importance for you to learn how to release stress.

Most goats possess an innate sense of timing. However, this is frequently rather slower than other people would like and when you are being harrassed or cajoled tensions begin to build. As a Saturn-ruled sign, it is essential that you recognize this and make those closest to you understand that you do things in your own good time and are frequently successful when others have tired themselves out pushing ahead too quickly. It is for this very reason that you rarely suffer from feverish conditions which can haunt the more energetic types. Despite this, it has to be said that you can neglect your own physical wellbeing. Luckily you are born under a durable sign, and are likely to live to a ripe old age. Routine and practical work provide you with security – a much-needed commodity for those born under this sign.

You have a tendency to become dogmatic and over-conscientious. Your attitude may be quite inflexible and rigidity of mind may lead to a rigid body. In order to avoid restriction of movement, you must learn to develop tolerance and flexibility and also to educate yourself not to take everything so much to heart.

The areas of the body ruled by your sign are the bones, knees, teeth, skin and skeletal system. There is a tendency for you to suffer from sluggish circulation, causing colds, arthritis and rheumatism. Dental problems and neuralgia often occur. Because of your tendency to worry, you are inclined to build up toxins which cause skin problems. You may also suffer from a nervous stomach. A well balanced diet can remove toxins and reflexology may help to prevent inhibition of movement.

As regards exercise, you should take up anything which keeps your movements fluid. Swimming is perhaps your best form of keeping fit, but any sports where joints can be easily damaged are best avoided.

When it comes to relaxing, you would benefit from deep breathing exercises and massage. Creative pastimes would release emotional inhibitions and prove to be extremely helpful. Aerobics would be fun as well as useful and dancing would help to keep your body supple even if it is only done in the privacy of your own room. Furthermore it allows a great release of tension. Remember that keeping fit needs to be fun as there is already too much seriousness in the other areas of your life.

When it comes to diet, you need plenty of dairy foods, citrus fruits, nuts, bran and yogurt. Increase your intake of these foods to remain healthy. Like your opposite sign of Cancer, you should never try to eat when you are upset.

Psychologically, you are too inclined to be preoccupied with the material world. Should you achieve power, and many of you do, you can find this a lonely position and you need to handle it wisely. Should you fail to achieve your aims you could become embittered. Not only is this an unpleasant characteristic, but it can also poison you by releasing toxins into your blood stream. In order to avoid this, it might be a good idea to set your sights lower. Alternatively, be content with achieving success in your personal life instead.

There is little doubt that one of your chief difficulties arises from your inhibitions and your inability to release emotion. It is almost as if you are frightened of knowing your true nature and would shrink from exploring it. Yet this is exactly what you need to do in order to remain fit and healthy and realize your full potential.

Remember that feelings which are controlled to freezing point can affect movement of the limbs. Tension is often indicated by the way that limbs are held and ultimately movement becomes restricted. All of this is avoidable if you are willing to follow at least some of the advice given here.

So how is your health likely to fare during the year? You will, of course, need to refer to the monthly guides for more in-depth study, but you must remember that Uranus is bouncing back and forth between your sign and Aquarius and you must find ways of easing this. Why not follow the advice above?

Over-indulgence is also likely in February, although of course you may decide that the ensuing hangover or tummy upset is a price worth paying. During the middle part of the year, your workload is likely to be heavier than usual and this too can lead to strain and stress. You need to know how to pace yourself sensibly during this period.

Mars' placing in your sign during December will make you more rash than usual and this could lead to minor mishaps with hot or sharp objects. Slow yourself down at this time and you will remain fit and healthy.

Throughout the entire year, your ruling planet Saturn will be in the sign of Pisces, suggesting that you may take cold whilst travelling. Therefore wrap up in inclement weather to maintain physical fitness.

Finally, although Capricorn tends to be something of a hypochondriac sign, in actual fact it is one of the fittest in the zodiac. With a little bit of care and caution, you are sure to live to a ripe old age.

Numerology Year

In order to discover the number of any year you are interested in, your 'individual year number', first take your birth date, day and month, and add this to the year you are interested in, be it in the past or in the future. As an example, say you were born on 9 August and you are interested in 1995:

$$
\begin{array}{r}
9 \\
8 \\
1995 \\
\hline
2012
\end{array}
$$

Then, write down $2 + 0 + 1 + 2$ and you will discover this equals 5. This means that the number of your year is 5.

You can experiment with this method by taking any year from your past and discovering with the help of the following guide whether or not numerology works out for you.

The guide is perennial and applicable to all Sun signs: you can look up years for your friends as well as for yourself. Use it to discover general trends ahead, the way you should be approaching a chosen period and how you can make the most of the future.

INDIVIDUAL YEAR NUMBER 1

GENERAL FEEL

A time for being more self-sufficient and one when you should be ready to grasp the nettle. All opportunities must be snapped up, after careful consideration. Also an excellent time for laying down the foundations for future success in all areas.

DEFINITION

Because this is the number 1 individual year, you will have the chance to start again in many areas of life. The emphasis will be upon the new; there will be fresh faces in your life, more opportunities and perhaps even new experiences. If you were born on either the 1st, 19th or 28th and were born under the sign of Aries or Leo then this will be an extremely important time. It is crucial during this cycle that you be prepared to go it alone, push back horizons and generally open up your mind. Time also for playing the leader or pioneer wherever necessary. If you have a hobby which you wish to turn into a business, or maybe you simply wish to introduce other people to your ideas and plans, then do so whilst experiencing this individual cycle. A great period too for laying down the plans for long-term future gains. Therefore, make sure you do your homework well and you will be reaping the rewards at a later date.

RELATIONSHIPS

This is an ideal period for forming new bonds, perhaps business relationships, new friends and new loves too. You will be attracted to those in high positions and with strong personalities. There may also be an emphasis on bonding with people a good deal younger than yourself. If you are already in a long-standing relationship, then it is time to clear away the dead wood between you which may have been causing misunderstandings and unhappiness. Whether in love or business, you will find those who are born under the sign of Aries, Leo or Aquarius far more common in your life, also those born on the following dates: 1st, 4th, 9th, 10th, 13th, 18th, 19th, 22nd and 28th. The most important months for this individual year when you are likely to meet up with those who have a strong influence on you are January, May, July and October.

CAREER

It is likely that you have been wanting to break free and to explore fresh horizons in your job or in your career and this is definitely a year for doing so. Because you are in a fighting mood, and because your decision-making qualities as well as your leadership qualities are foremost, it will be an easy matter for you to find assistance as well as to impress other people. Major professional changes are likely and you will also feel more independent within your existing job. Should you want times for making important career moves, then choose Mondays or Tuesdays. These are good days for pushing your luck and presenting your ideas well. Changes connected with your career are going to be more likely during April, May, July and September.

HEALTH

If you have forgotten the name of your doctor or dentist, then this is the year for going for check-ups. A time too when people of a certain age are likely to start wearing glasses. The emphasis seems to be on eyes. Start a good health regime. This will help you cope with any adverse events that almost assuredly lie ahead. The important months for your own health as well as for loved ones are March, May and August.

INDIVIDUAL YEAR NUMBER 2

GENERAL FEEL

You will find it far easier to relate to other people.

DEFINITION

What you will need during this cycle is diplomacy, cooperation and the ability to put yourself in someone else's shoes. Whatever you began last year will now begin to show signs of progress. However, don't expect miracles; changes are going to be slow rather than at the speed of light. Changes will be taking place all around you. It is possible too that you will be considering moving from one area to another, maybe even to another country. There is a lively feel about domesticity and in relationships with the opposite sex too. This is going to be a marvellous year for making things come true and asking for favours. However, on no account should you force yourself and your opinions on other people. A spoonful of honey is going to get you a good deal further than a spoonful of vinegar. If you are born under the sign of Cancer or Taurus, or if your birthday falls on the 2nd, 11th, 20th or 29th, then this year is going to be full of major events.

RELATIONSHIPS

You need to associate with other people far more than is usually the case – perhaps out of necessity. The emphasis is on love, friendship and professional partnerships. The opposite sex will be much more prepared to get involved in your life than is normally the case. This is a year your chances of becoming engaged or married are increased and there is likely to be expansion in your family in the form of a lovely addition and also in the families of your friends and those closest to you. The instinctive and caring side to your personality is going to be strong and very obvious. You will quickly discover that you will be extra touchy and sensitive to things that other people say. Further, you will find those born under the sign of Cancer, Taurus and Libra entering your life far more than is usually the case. This also applies to those who are born on the 2nd, 6th, 7th, 11th, 15th, 20th, 24th, 25th or 29th of the month.

Romantic and family events are likely to be emphasized during April, June and September.

CAREER

There is a strong theme of change here, but there is no point in having a panic attack about that because, after all, life is about change. However, in this particular individual year any transformation or upheaval is likely to be of an internal nature, such as at your place of work, rather than external. You may find your company is moving from one area to another, or perhaps there are changes between departments. Quite obviously then the most important thing for you to do in order to make your life easy is to be adaptable. There is a strong possibility too that you may be given added responsibility. Do not flinch, this will bring in extra reward.

If you are thinking of searching for employment this year, then try to arrange all meetings and negotiations on Monday and Friday. These are good days for asking for favours or rises too. The best months are March, April, June, August, and December. All these are important times for change.

HEALTH

This individual cycle emphasizes stomach problems. The important thing for you is to eat sensibly, rather than going on, for example, a crash diet – which could be detrimental. If you are female then you would be wise to have a check-up at least once during the year ahead just to be sure you can continue to enjoy good health. All should be discriminating when dining out. Check cutlery, and take care if food has only been partially cooked. Furthermore, emotional stress could get you down, but only if you allow it. Provided you set aside some periods of relaxation in each day when you can close your eyes and let everything drift away then you will have little to worry about. When it comes to diet, be sure that the emphasis is on nutrition, rather than fighting the flab. Perhaps it would be a good idea to become less weight conscious during this period and let your body find its natural ideal weight on its own. The months of February, April, July and November may show health changes in some way. Commonsense is your best guide during this year.

INDIVIDUAL YEAR NUMBER 3

GENERAL FEEL

You are going to be at your most creative and imaginative during this time. There is a theme of expansion and growth and you will want to polish up your self-image in order to make the 'big impression'.

DEFINITION

It is a good year for reaching out, for expansion. Social and artistic developments should be interesting as well as profitable and this will help to promote happiness. There will be a strong urge in you to improve yourself, either your image or your reputation or perhaps your mind. Your popularity soars through the ceiling and this delights you. Involving yourself with something creative brings increased success plus a good deal of satisfaction. However, it is imperative that you keep yourself in a positive mood. This will attract attention and appreciation of all of your talents. Projects which were begun two years ago are likely to be sprouting this year. If you are born under the sign of Pisces or Sagittarius, or your birthday falls on the 3rd, 12th, 21st or 30th, then this year is going to be particularly special and successful.

RELATIONSHIPS

There is a happy-go-lucky feel about all your relationships and you are in a flirty, fancy-free mood. Heaven help anyone trying to catch you during the next twelve months: they will need to get their skates on. Relationships are likely to be ethereal and fun rather than heavy going. It is possible too that you will find yourself with those who are younger than yourself, particularly those born under the signs of Pisces and Sagittarius, and those whose birth dates add up to 3, 6 or 9. Your individual cycle shows important months for relationships are March, May, August and December.

CAREER

As I discussed earlier, this individual number is one that suggests branching out and personal growth, so be ready to take on anything new. Not surprisingly, your career aspects look bright and shiny. You are definitely going to be more ambitious and must keep up that positive façade and attract opportunities. Avoid taking obligations too flippantly; it is important that you adopt a conscientious approach to all your responsibilities. You may take on a fresh course of learning or look for a new job, and the important days for doing so would be on Thursday and Friday: these are definitely your best days. This is particularly true in the months of February, March, May, July and November: expect expansion in your life and take a chance during these times.

HEALTH

Because you are likely to be out and about painting the town all the colours of the rainbow, it is likely that some of your health problems could come through over-indulgence or perhaps tiredness. However, if you have got to have some health problems, I suppose these are the best ones to experience, because they are under your control. There is also a possibility that you may get a little fraught over work, which may result in some emotional scenes. However, you are sensible enough to realize they should not be taken too seriously. If you are prone to skin allergies, then these too could be giving you problems during this particular year. The best advice you can follow is not to go to extremes that will affect your body or your mind. It is all very well to have fun, but after a while too much not only affects your health but also the degree of enjoyment you experience. Take extra care between January and March, and June and October, especially where these are winter months for you.

INDIVIDUAL YEAR NUMBER 4

GENERAL FEEL

It is back to basics this year. Do not build on shaky foundations. Get yourself organized and be prepared to work a little harder than you usually do and you will come through without any great difficulty.

DEFINITION

It is imperative this year that you have a grand plan. Do not simply rush off without considering the consequences and avoid dabbling of all descriptions. It is likely too that you will be gathering more responsibility and on occasions this could lead you to feeling unappreciated, claustrophobic and perhaps over-burdened in some ways. Although it is true to say that this cycle in your individual life tends to bring about a certain amount of limitation, whether this be on the personal side to life, the psychological or the financial, you now have the chance to get yourself together and to build on more solid foundations. Security is definitely your key word at this time. When it comes to any project, or job or plan, it is important that you ask the right questions. In other words, do your homework before you go off half cock. That would be a disaster. If you are an Aquarius, a Leo or a Gemini or you are born on the 4th, 13th, 22nd, or the 31st of any month, this individual year will be extremely important and long remembered.

RELATIONSHIPS

You will find that it is the eccentric, the unusual, the unconventional, the downright odd, that will be drawn into your life during this particular cycle. It is also strongly possible that people you have not met for some time may be re-entering your circle and an older person or somebody outside your own social or perhaps religious background will be drawn to you too. When it comes to the romantic side of things, again you are drawn to that which is different from usual. You may even form a relationship with someone who comes from a totally different background, perhaps from a distance. Something unusual about them stimulates and excites you. Gemini, Leo and Aquarius are your likely favourites, as well as anyone whose birth number adds up to 1, 4, 5, or 7. Certainly the most exciting months for romance are going to be February, April, July and November. Make sure then that you put yourself about during this particular time, and be ready for literally anything.

CAREER

Once more we have the theme of the unusual and different in this area of life. You may be plodding along in the same old rut when suddenly lightning strikes and you find yourself besieged by offers from other people and in a panic, not quite sure what to do. There may be a period when nothing particular seems to be going on, when to your astonishment you are given some promotion or some exciting challenge to take on board. Literally anything can happen in this particular cycle of your life. The individual year 4 also inclines towards added responsibilities and it is important that you do not offload them on to other people or cringe in fear. They will eventually pay off and in the meantime you will be gaining in experience and paving the way for greater success in the future. When you want to arrange any kind of meeting, negotiation or perhaps ask for any kind of favour at work, then try to do so on a Monday or a Wednesday for the luckiest results. January, February, April, October and November are certainly the months when you must play the opportunist and be ready to say yes to anything that comes your way.

HEALTH

The biggest problems that you will have to face this year are caused by stress, so it is important that you attend to your diet and are as philosophical as possible as well as ready to adapt to changing conditions. You are likely to find that people you thought you knew well are acting out of character and this throws you off balance. Take care too when visiting the doctor. Remember that you are dealing with a human being and that doctors, like the rest of us, can make mistakes.

Unless you are 100 per cent satisfied then go for a second opinion over anything important. Try to be sceptical about yourself too because you are going to be a good deal more moody than usual. The times that need special attention are February, May, September and November. If any of these months fall in the winter part of your year, then wrap up well and dose up on vitamin C.

INDIVIDUAL YEAR NUMBER 5

GENERAL FEEL

There will be many more opportunities for you to get out and about and travel is certainly going to be playing a large part in your year. Change too must be expected and even embraced – after all, it is part of life. You will have more free time and choices, so all in all things look promising.

DEFINITION

It is possible that you tried previously to get something off the launching pad but for one reason or another, it simply didn't happen. Luckily, you now get a chance to renew those old plans and put them into action. You are certainly going to feel that things are changing for the better in all areas. You are going to be more actively involved with the public and will enjoy a certain amount of attention and publicity. You may have failed in the past but this year mistakes will be easier to accept and learn from, and you are going to find yourself both physically and mentally more in tune with your environment and with those you care about than ever before. If you are a Gemini or a Virgo or are born on the 5th,

14th or 23rd then this is going to be a period of major importance for you and you must be ready to take advantage of this.

RELATIONSHIPS

Lucky you! Your sexual magnetism goes through the ceiling and you will be involved in many relationships during the year ahead. You have that extra charisma about you which will be drawing others to you and you can look forward to being choosy. There will be an inclination to be drawn to those who are considerably younger than yourself. It is likely too that you will find that those born under the signs of Taurus, Gemini, Virgo and Libra as well as those whose birth date adds up to 2, 5 or 6 will play an important part in your year. The months for attracting others in a big way are January, March, June, October and December.

CAREER

This is considered by all numerologists as being one of the best numbers for self-improvement in all areas, and particularly on the professional front. It will be relatively easy for you to sell your ideas and yourself as well as to push your skills and expertise under the noses of other people. They will certainly sit up and notice. Clearly, then, a time for you to view the world as though it were your oyster and to get out there and grab your slice of the action. You have increased confidence and should be able to get exactly what you want. Friday and Wednesday are perhaps the best days if looking for a job or going to negotiations or interviews, or in fact for generally pushing yourself into the limelight. Watch out for March, May, September, October or December. Something of great importance could pop up at this time. There will certainly be a chance for advancement; whether you take it up or not is of course entirely up to you.

HEALTH

Getting a good night's rest could be your problem during the year ahead, since that mind of yours is positively buzzing and won't let you rest. Try turning your brain off at bedtime, otherwise you will finish up irritable and exhausted. Try to take things a step at a time without rushing around. Meditation may help you to relax and do more for your physical wellbeing than anything else. Because this is an extremely active year, you will need to do some careful planning so that you can cope with ease rather than rushing around like a demented mayfly. Furthermore, try to avoid going over the top with alcohol, food, sex, gambling or anything which could be described as 'get rich quick'. During January, April, August, and October, watch yourself a bit, you could do with some coddling, particularly if these happen to be winter months for you.

INDIVIDUAL YEAR NUMBER 6

GENERAL FEEL

There is likely to be increased responsibility and activity within your domestic life. There will be many occasions when you will be helping loved ones and your sense of duty is going to be strong.

DEFINITION

Activities for the most part are likely to be centred around property, family, loved ones, romance and your home. Your artistic appreciation will be good and you will be drawn to anything that is colourful and beautiful, and possessions that have a strong appeal to your eye or even your ear. Where domesticity is concerned, there is a strong suggestion that you may move out of one home into another. This is an excellent time too for self-education, for branching out, for graduating, for taking on some extra courses – whether simply to improve your appearance or to improve your mind. When it comes to your social life you are inundated with chances to attend social functions, such as openings of art galleries and facilities. You are going to be the real social butterfly flitting from scene to scene and enjoying yourself thoroughly. Try to accept nine out of ten invitations that come your way because they bring with them chances of advancement. If you are born on the 6th, 15th or 24th or should your birth sign be Taurus, Libra or Cancer then this is going to be a year that will be long remembered as a very positive one.

RELATIONSHIPS

When it comes to love, sex and romance the individual year 6 is perhaps the most successful. It is a time for being swept off your feet, for becoming engaged or for getting married. On the more negative side, perhaps there is separation and divorce. However the latter can be avoided, provided you are prepared to sit down and communicate properly. There is an emphasis too on pregnancy and birth, or changes in existing relationships. Circumstances will be sweeping you along. If you are born under the sign of Taurus, Cancer or Libra, then it is even more likely that this will be a major year for you, as well as for those born on dates adding up to 6, 3 or 2. The most memorable months of your year are going to be February, May,

September and November. Grab all opportunities to enjoy yourself and improve your relationships during these periods.

CAREER

A good year for this side to life too, with the chances of promotion and recognition for past efforts all coming your way. You will be able to improve your position in life even though lately it is likely you have been frustrated. On the cash front big rewards will come flooding in mainly because you are prepared to fulfil your obligations and commitments without complaint or protest. Other people will appreciate all the efforts you have put in, so plod along and you will find your efforts will not be in vain. Perversely, if you are looking for a job or setting up an interview, negotiation or a meeting, or simply want to advertise your talents in some way, then your best days for doing so are Monday, Thursday and Friday. Long-term opportunities are very strong during the months of February, April, August, September and November. These are the key periods for pushing yourself up the ladder of success.

HEALTH

If you are to experience any problems of a physical nature during this year, then they could be tied up with the throat, nose or the tonsils plus the upper parts of the body. Basically what you need to stay healthy during this year is plenty of sunlight, moderate exercise, fresh air and changes of scene. Escape to the coast too if this is at all possible. The months for being particularly watchful are March, July, September and December. Think twice before doing anything during this time and there is no reason why you shouldn't stay hale and hearty for the whole year.

INDIVIDUAL YEAR NUMBER 7

GENERAL FEEL

A year for inner growth and for finding out what really makes you tick and what you need to make you happy. Self-awareness and discovery are all emphasized during the individual year 7.

DEFINITION

You will be provided with the opportunity to place as much emphasis as possible on your personal life and your own wellbeing. There will be many occasions when you will find yourself analysing your past motives and actions, and developing a need to give more attention to your own personal needs, goals and desires. There will also be many occasions when you will feel the need to escape any kind of confusion, muddle or noise, and time spent alone will not be wasted. It will give you time for meditation and also for examining exactly where you have come to so far and where you want to go in the future. It is important you make up your mind what you want out of this particular year because once you have done this you will attain those ambitions. Failure to do so could mean you end up chasing your tail and that is a pure waste of time and energy. You will also discover that secrets about yourself and other people could be surfacing during this year. If you are born under the sign of Pisces or Cancer, or on the 7th, 16th or 25th of the month, then this year will be especially wonderful.

RELATIONSHIPS

It has to be said from the word go that this is not the best year for romantic interest. A strong need for contemplation will mean spending time on your own. Any romance that does develop this year may not live up to your great expectations, but, providing you are prepared to take things as they come without jumping to conclusions, then you will enjoy yourself without getting hurt. Decide exactly what it is you have in mind and then go for it. Romantic interests this year are likely to be with people who are born on dates that add up to 2, 4 or 7 or with people born under the sign of Cancer or Pisces. Watch for romantic opportunities during January, April, August and October.

CAREER

When we pass through this particular individual cycle, two things in life tend to occur: retirement from the limelight, or a general slowing down, perhaps by taking leave of absence or maybe retraining in some way. It is likely too that you will become more aware of your own occupational expertise and skills – you will begin to understand your true purpose in life and will feel much more enlightened. Long sought-after goals begin to come to life if you have been drifting of late. The best attitude to have throughout the year is an exploratory one when it comes to your work. If you want to set up negotiations, interviews or meetings, arrange them for Monday or Friday. In fact any favours you seek should be tackled on these days. January, March, July, August, October and December are particularly good for self-advancement.

HEALTH

Since, in comparison to previous years, this is a rather quiet time, health problems are likely to be minor. Some will possibly come through irritation or worry and the best thing to do is to attempt to remain meditative and calm. This state of mind will bring positive results. Failure to do so may create unnecessary problems by allowing your imagination to run completely out of

control. You need time this year to restore, recuperate
and contemplate. Any health changes that do occur
are likely to happen in February, June, August and
November.

INDIVIDUAL YEAR NUMBER 8

GENERAL FEEL

This is going to be a time for success, for making
important moves and changes, a time when you may
gain power and certainly one when your talents are
going to be recognized.

DEFINITION

This individual year gives you the chance to 'think big',
a time you can occupy the limelight and wield power. If
you were born on the 8th, 17th or 26th of the month or
come under the sign of Capricorn, pay attention to this
year and make sure you make the most of it. You should
develop greater maturity and will discover a true feeling
of faith and destiny, both in yourself and in events that
occur. This is a cycle connected with career, ambition
and money, but debts from the past will have to be
re-paid. For example, an old responsibility or debt that
you may have avoided in past years may reappear to
haunt you. However, whatever you do with this twelve
months, aim high – think big, think success and above
all be positive.

RELATIONSHIPS

This particular individual year is one which is strongly
connected with birth, divorce and marriage – most of
the landmarks we experience in life in fact. Lovewise,
those who are more experienced or older than you,
or someone of power, authority, influence or wealth

will be very attractive. This year will be putting you back in touch with those from your past – old friends, comrades, associates, and even romances from long ago crop up once more. You should not experience any great problems romantically this year, especially if you are dealing with Capricorns or Librans, or with those whose date of birth adds up to 8, 6 or 3. The best months for romance to develop are likely to be March, July, September and December.

CAREER

The number 8 year is generally believed to be the best one when it comes to bringing in cash. It is also good for asking for a rise or achieving promotion or authority over other people. This is your year for bathing in the limelight of success, the result perhaps of your past efforts. Now you will be rewarded. Financial success is all but guaranteed, provided you keep faith with your ambitions and yourself. It is important that you set major aspirations for yourself and work slowly towards them. You will be surprised how easily they are fulfilled. Conversely, if you are looking for work, then do set up interviews, negotiations and meetings, preferably on Saturday, Thursday or Friday, which are your luckiest days. Also watch out for chances to do yourself a bit of good during February, June, July, September and November.

HEALTH

You can avoid most health problems, particularly head-aches, constipation or liver problems, by avoiding moods of depression, and feelings of loneliness. It is important when these descend that you keep yourself busy enough not to dwell on them. When it comes to receiving attention from the medical profession you would be well advised to get a second opinion. Eat wisely, try to keep a positive and enthusiastic outlook on life and all will be well. Periods which need special care are January, May, July and October. Therefore, if these months fall during the winter part of your year, wrap up and dose yourself with vitamins.

INDIVIDUAL YEAR NUMBER 9

GENERAL FEEL

A time for tying up the loose ends. Wishes are likely to be fulfilled and matters brought to swift conclusions. Inspirations run amok. Much travel is likely.

DEFINITION

The number 9 individual year is perhaps the most successful of all. It tends to represent the completion of matters and affairs, whether in work, business, or personal affairs. Your ability to let go of habits, people and negative circumstances or situations, that may have been holding you back, is strong. The sympathetic and humane side to your character also surfaces and you learn to give more freely of yourself without expecting anything in return. Any good deeds that you do will certainly be well rewarded, in terms of satisfaction and perhaps financially too. If you are born under the sign of Aries or Scorpio, or on the 9th, 18th or 27th of the month, this is certainly going to be an all important year.

RELATIONSHIPS

The individual year 9 is a cycle which gives appeal as well as influence. Because of this, you will be getting emotionally tied up with members of the opposite sex who may be outside your usual cultural or ethnic group. The reason for this is that this particular number relates to humanity and of course this tends to quash ignorance, pride and bigotry. You also discover that Aries, Leo and Scorpio people are going to be much more evident in your domestic affairs, as well as those whose birth dates add up to 9, 3 or 1. The important months for relationships are February, June, August and November. These will be extremely hectic and eventful from a romantic viewpoint and there are times when you could be swept off your feet.

CAREER

This is a year which will help to make many of your dreams and ambitions come true. Furthermore it is an excellent time for success if you are involved in marketing your skills, your talents and your expertise on a broader level. You may be thinking of expanding abroad for example and if so this is certainly a good idea. You will find that harmony and cooperation with your co-workers or those who work for you are easier than before and this will help your dreams and ambitions. The best days for you if you want to line up meetings or negotiations are going to be Tuesday and Thursday and this also applies if you are looking for employment or want a special day for doing something of an ambitious nature. Employment or business changes could also feature during January, May, June, August and October.

HEALTH

The only physical problem you may have during this particular year is accidents, so be careful. Try too to avoid unnecessary tension and arguments with other people. Take extra care when you are on the roads: no drinking and driving for example. You will only have problems if you play your own worst enemy. Be extra watchful when in the kitchen or bathroom: sharp instruments that you find in these areas can lead to cuts being commonplace, unless you take care.

Monthly Guide

JANUARY

Firstly it is important to remind you about the lesson you are supposed to be learning up until August. It appears that you have learned how to establish yourself on a wider basis by harnessing your emotional capacities in some form of creative expression, either by having children or through hobbies and the pursuit of pleasure in general. Now it is time to project yourself, perhaps in a colourful career. It is time too when your status is likely to be increasing, both at work and in your local community. As an ambitious sign, you will appreciate the fact that now the stars are encouraging you to pursue your ambitions – and with determination you can succeed.

This month there are three planets, namely the Sun, Uranus and Neptune, in your sign. This then is very much a period for self-advancement and it will pay you to keep a high profile. Regardless of what is important to you, push ahead in an effort to achieve your goals.

It is certainly a time when self-employed or freelance workers can do a great deal to generate interest in their talents or business. Avoid the tendency to be too introspective. Instead channel your energies outwards and obviously try to throw off inhibitions which could have an adverse effect on your health as well as stifle your progress in life. Although you may not be as flamboyant as Leo or as expressive as Gemini, you have a lot to offer in the way of endurance, reliability and practical common sense. All of these can lead to your ultimate success.

The rays of the Sun should help to fill you with confidence. This in turn should help you to cast away negative thinking and make sensible plans for the future, which with your tenacity and determination are sure to materialize at some point.

If you need a time for travelling, looking for work or attending to legal matters, then choose the first week of the month when Mercury is in your sign. Minor changes can also be undertaken successfully at this time.

Mercury's move into Aquarius on 7 January is likely to bring financial gains through advertising, publishing, journalism, agencies and travel. Nevertheless, there is likely to be a rapid turnover and you will need to ensure that you can cover your expenses. Luckily your financial skill is already quite awesome and this is encouraged during this month. It is a time too when you will be valuing things by their immediate usefulness. If you collect anything, especially books, you are likely to be adding to your collection.

Up until 23 January, Mars will be in the sign of Virgo, encouraging independent thought and enabling you to fight for your convictions. Heaven help anyone who gets in your way once you have decided you are right. Workwise, the most hectic period is likely to be during the last week of the month when Mars enters the zenith of your chart. At this time your energy will be inexhaustible and you must avoid taking on too much. You will be resolute, independent and are likely to find success through enterprise. Just for once you will be very much living in the present. However, do not allow yourself to become embroiled in arguments and debates at work.

Socially you are likely to be at your most fun-loving during the first week when Venus occupies the sign of Scorpio. At this time you will be affectionate, fond of company, and will find happiness through friends, clubs and societies. It is likely too that you will be drawn to the more sensitive and artistic members of your group. Regardless of your sex, you will find the company of females more than usually rewarding.

Romantically, the first week of the month may be fun but fairly casual, but after this you need to guard against behaviour which could cause something of a scandal. In order to avoid this, it would be a good idea to check on all those you become involved with. Someone may not be as honest with you as they should be. You have no wish to deceive anybody as it simply is not in your character to do so. As it is, you tend to worry over the slightest thing and you do not actively seek out trouble. Quite obviously then, this month tends to favour those of you already in steady relationships. Therefore do not allow yourself to be led into temptation which is so easy to avoid.

Healthwise, apart from being a little tense and easily exhausted during the first week, you should remain hale and hearty at this time. However, do ensure that you set aside periods for real relaxation when you must let the whole world drift away.

Now let us look at the state of the Moon. The new Moon this month occurs on January 1 which certainly augurs well for you as it occurs in your sign. You are provided then with a couple of days in which to make changes, start new projects, change your image and be as adventurous as you possibly can be. Throw off past cares, having learned their lessons, and look forward to a brighter and more carefree future.

The full Moon on 16 January occurs in your opposite sign of Cancer. This could be resurrecting hidden feelings in one of your relationships and you need to tread rather carefully with the emotions of other people. Certainly do not neglect loved ones at this time or you will be asking for trouble. A little bit of forethought can take you a long way at this time.

Fortunately we are blessed with a second new Moon this month. It occurs in the sign of Aquarius on the 30th and influences the financial area of your life. Many of you will be calling in money which is owed or perhaps generating a fresh source of income. Certainly this is an ideal time for financial meetings and generally pushing your luck on a practical level.

This then can be a productive and positive start to the new year.

FEBRUARY

For most of this month, the Sun will be influencing the financial area of your life. This is likely to bring gain through government bodies, influential people and maybe male members of your family. Certainly money will be coming in more easily than it has been for some time and you must make sure that it stays there rather than letting it drift out on extravagance. This placing will be encouraging your generosity, your ambitions, your reserves of strength and also your attraction to splendour. It is an excellent time for trying to generate interest in your talents and also to raise money. You will find that people such as bank managers will be only too willing to back your ideas as they are sound and practical. However, it is not a time when you will be prepared to do anything for nothing. You will be anxious to be recompensed for any efforts you put out on behalf of other people. Mercury will also be influencing the financial area of your life. It is in retrograde movement until 17 February which means that from our position in space it appears to be going backwards. It will not be a good idea for you to involve yourself in matters related to travel, advertising, publishing, journalism or agencies until after this date. Try then to avoid signing contracts until the 17th. Once this date has passed, you can push ahead in all areas. Your financial skill will be increased and you will be valuing things by their immediate usefulness.

On a more personal level, Venus is in your sign from 5 February onwards. This suggests that you will be more affectionate than usual, harmony-seeking, pleasant, cheerful, sociable, sympathetic, honest, artistic and fond of appreciation. Certainly then, this should be a great time for those of you with creative skills and you must not hesitate to present your ideas and suggestions to other people. Healthwise, Venus brings good health and good looks, although there may be a tendency for you to over-indulge on occasions. However, your constitution seems to be strong enough to take the extra onslaught.

Romantically, you can hardly go wrong this month. You are not only looking good but feeling good, and you are attracting in a big way. Any partnership or relationship formed during this particular month is sure to be lucky for you. Furthermore you will be more prepared to work harder at sorting out any differences between yourself and loved ones.

If you have been considering forming a professional partnership for some time, then that time has arrived. Push ahead with confidence, not only in yourself but also in the other person.

During the latter part of the month, your head will be positively bursting with ideas and it would be wise to keep a pen and paper in readiness so that you can jot them down otherwise they could be lost.

Mar's move into the sign of Leo will be extremely helpful for those of you involved in any kind of research. However, you should strenuously try to avoid getting into any kind of strife or argument with people in positions of power or influence such as officials.

Socially you are in great demand and should snap up all invitations that come your way. Not only could they lead to romance if you are single, but also to interesting contacts that can help you in your professional life.

February, then, seems to have a great deal going for it and it is up to you as usual to make the most of it.

Now let us look at the state of the Moon. Regrettably, because we were spoiled with two new Moons last month, this month we are left solely with the full Moon which occurs on 15 February in the sign of Leo. This is the one time in the month when you may allow yourself to be brought down by the criticism of other people. At this time, draw on your Capricorn strength and resist any attempt to undermine you. You are on the right track, Capricorn. You know it and I know it, so do not allow yourself to doubt it for one moment.

MARCH

The position of the Sun in Pisces up until 21 March will be broadening your mind, making you more impartial, creative, self-reliant, cheerful, lively, accomplished and constructive. You will be taking any opportunity to travel, although this is likely only to be short visits. Nevertheless they will be stimulating. It is likely too that relationships with relatives and neighbours will be running more smoothly and that you will be receiving invitations from them. Those of you who are involved in education are likely to find study successful. All of you will feel a strong need to spread knowledge wherever you can.

During the first half of this month, Mercury will continue to influence your finances, making this a lucky time for those of you involved in advertising, publishing, journalism or agency work. Your financial skills will be obvious for all to see. You can expect people to come to you for advice and you will feel flattered. From 15 March onwards, Mercury moves into Aries. This will certainly stimulate your mind, and you will be more alert, studious, busy and versatile. You will be much more able to cope with any changes that may be taking place, although they are likely to be minor. You will be finding little excuses to go on short trips. These will be very stimulating to you and will help you to make casual contact with other people.

You are likely to feel an innate need to expand your mind and you may undertake a new course of training or learning that will be useful as well as profitable in the near future.

It is likely that you will be hearing from brothers or sisters who perhaps live some distance from home. The news will be welcome and will help to boost your morale. You are likely to be looking forward to a reunion in the near future.

Venus will be moving into the financial area of life on 3 March. Regardless of your sex, you may benefit from the ideas of females. You may also gain from artistic pursuits, and perhaps you will be spoiling yourself with a minor luxury. Those of you who need assistance from other people will find it readily available. This is a time when you can expect a good income and you will be using your possessions and appearance to your best advantage. If you are out of work you will be making a big impression at this time.

Socially, you will be prepared to travel further than

usual for the sake of enjoyment and may be visiting those you have neglected for quite some time. Invitations will be coming in from those who live close to you and small impromptu get-togethers are likely this month.

Sexually, the adrenalin certainly seems to be pounding through your veins and physical attraction will be the norm. However, guard against impulse and be your usual self. In other words, play it safe.

Romantically, it seems to be those who are in a steady relationship who will find the greatest comfort and security during the month ahead, although the last week brings with it the possibility of brief encounters which you may care to develop at a later date.

Certainly this is a month when other people will be appreciating all your efforts, both in your personal life and at work, particularly where creativity is concerned. For once you will allow yourself to be emotionally swayed by situations and will find the right combination of feelings and practicality when it comes to problem solving.

Pluto's retrograde movement in the area related to friends and contacts points to the fact that you will feel the need for friendship and may be drawn to those who are somewhat idealistic as well as influential. Remember that although this is a good time for asking favours as other people are ready to assist, they may, through no fault of their own, be unable to provide everything they promise. Nevertheless, any help they do give is sure to be positive and constructive as well as useful for your future advancement.

Now let us look at the state of the Moon. The new Moon falls in the sign of Pisces on 1 March, stirring up your imagination, adaptability and common sense. This will be extremely useful for those of you who are involved with studies. This is an excellent period too for

short visits or trips and will prove particularly successful
for people involved with sales.

The full Moon in Virgo on 17 March suggests that if it
should become necessary for you to travel any distance,
then it would be a good idea to double-check on all
arrangements in order to avoid any kind of confusion.

Luckily we are blessed with a second new Moon this
month on the 31st in the sign of Aries. This will certainly
be stirring up your emotions as well as your intuition
and you are likely to come across as a softer, warmer
human being which will be extremely attractive to the
opposite sex. As always with a new Moon, this is a great
time for starting anything new. This includes changes
of direction, ideas or appearance.

March will be a lively month, and one which seems
to contain a good deal of opportunity. It is up to you to
make the most of it.

APRIL

During April, the Sun will be in the sign of Aries up
until the 21st. You will certainly be taking a great deal
of pride and pleasure in the company of your family and
also in your home. Many of you will be improving your
surroundings and money spent to this end will not go
to waste.

This time is particularly useful for those of you
involved in property matters and all its allied trades.
It is also good for sorting out differences within the
family in a stable, practical but sensitive way. Disagreements with parents can be sorted out without
too much difficulty. Because the Sun is accompanied
by Mercury in this area, there is sure to be a good deal
of activity going on at home. For some of you, this could

mean that you are stepping up your home entertaining activities, while for others there is a possibility of mental study going on at home – perhaps you are working for exams or attempting to improve yourself in some way.

Many of you will decide that it is time to move on and you could be looking at potential new homes.

Venus' placing in Pisces increases your artistic appreciation and resurrects the bright, hopeful and harmonious side to your character. It is a particularly lucky time for those of you who work in the media or who travel on a professional basis. In moments of doubt, you will find that friends and those who live close by will be only too willing to lend a helping hand and this will certainly warm that chilly heart of yours.

Your mental attitude this month is certainly positive but charming, firm but adaptable.

Uranus enters the financial area of life on 2 April and this seems to suggest that over the next couple of months you will be gaining from unusual sources. If you are interested in antiques, you could be picking up a bargain. Some of you may even experience a windfall. Should a financial crisis arise, try not to fret as you will be able to extricate yourself through your own ingenuity.

At the moment you seem to be able to distinguish between your emotions and your sexual feelings. Your physical appetites are on the increase and because of this you may find them totally disconnected from the way you feel. Be your usual commonsense self and there will be no problems at all, unless of course you are in a steady relationship, in which case make strenuous efforts to bridge any gap that you may feel exists otherwise it could turn into a yawning chasm. This is avoidable and entirely up to you. If you are fancy-free, then Venus' position in Pisces will be encouraging many brief encounters. You are in a flirtatious and flighty mood and will be reluctant to settle down with anyone. You will view each member of the opposite sex with interest and you will be keen to know what they think and feel, rather than simply focusing on the way they look.

Jupiter in Sagittarius goes into retrograde movement on 2 April, which means that from our position in space it appears to be going backwards. Because of this, do not trust too much to instinct. Now is the time when you will need your practical common sense and must not be led astray by confused feelings.

Healthwise, there seems to be little to worry you, although if you are feeling under the weather or have forgotten the name of your dentist, then it would be a good idea to go for a check-up as prevention is always better than cure.

April contains many opportunities for you to improve yourself and your position in life. Because you seem to be thinking only positive thoughts, you can make a great deal of progress throughout this period. Be sure to avoid the company of those who damp your spirits. Socialize only with those who offer encouragement or those who can introduce a little humour into your existence.

Now let us turn to the state of the Moon. The full Moon this month occurs in the sign of Libra on the 15th. This is, of course, the zenith of your chart and it suggests you will easily be making social contact with other people. You will be meeting many acquaintances and your popularity does not seem to be in question. However, avoid making any new beginnings on a professional level for the time being, as full Moons are ideally used for putting the finishing touches to projects, rather than proceeding with new ideas.

The new Moon this month occurs in the sign of Taurus on the 29th. You are likely to experience a couple of days then when you will indulge in a constant search for pleasure. Emotionally you could be rather fickle and difficult to please and therefore this will be a flirtatious time. Certainly you are provided with a couple of great days if you are at all artistic. Now is the time for presenting your ideas and projects to other people as they are sure to receive a warm welcome. Should you be in a steady relationship at this time, you will be expecting and receiving a good deal of attention.

You seem to have a good deal to look forward to during April and you must continue to banish pessimism, negative thinking and situations and people that bring you down.

MAY

May seems to hold a great deal of promise. On a professional level, it is particularly good for the sportsperson, those who work with animals or those whose work involves creativity. Your power to give and receive enjoyment and pleasure is on the increase too. You will certainly be throwing yourself whole-heartedly into the social whirl. Any chances to go to parties or other special occasions should be snapped up without further ado. For once make relaxation and socializing as important to you as your ambitions and work.

Venus remains in the property and home area of life for the first eighteen days of this month, therefore a great deal of fun can be had in the company of your family and also at home. However, once this date has passed, you will be enjoying theatre-going and entertainments in a big way. This is a month for sheer enjoyment, and even a little bit of self-indulgence. It is true that you may be dramatizing yourself a little but this characteristic is unlikely to be upsetting those closest to you.

Romantically, you are at your most flirtatious, and should you be fancy-free, you will certainly be reluctant to settle down with any one partner. Even though there is a strong possibility that you could meet someone special, it is unlikely that you will recognize this fact until this month has expired when life becomes a little quieter.

Where the family is concerned, if you are a parent then you will find your children much more affectionate than usual and you will be providing entertainment for them which you will also enjoy.

Financially, you may be damaging your bank account a little because entertainment and socializing seem to be more important than usual. Nevertheless, money invested in this way will be worthwhile, just as long as you do not become too luxury-minded.

If money is owed to you, then chase it seriously during the first week as people who are in your debt will be elusive and evasive after this time.

Healthwise, Mercury's placing in Gemini could resurrect in you an interest in hygiene or health matters. There may also be a tendency for you to become exhausted rather more easily, but bearing in mind your hectic social life this is not at all surprising.

It is likely too that you will be meeting new people and you may develop an interest in technical matters. You could decide to retrain in some way.

When it comes to tackling anything new or making world-shattering decisions, do so before Mercury moves into retrograde action on 24 May. After this date things could become unnecessarily complicated, so why make life difficult for yourself?

Now let us look at the state of the Moon. The full Moon this month occurs in Scorpio on the 14th, making this a time when you will easily form social contacts and may even be extra popular. However, unless you exercise

that wonderful Capricorn caution, you may discover
that some of these characters are a little unreliable. Do
not become embroiled in scandal-mongering or gossip
or it could rebound on you at a later date. Take care
too how you handle existing friends, as a wrong word
could frighten them off as they are extra sensitive at the
moment.

The new Moon this month appears in Gemini on
the 29th. This suggests minor new beginnings where
work matters are concerned and plenty of news from
colleagues. If you have been feeling under the weather
recently, you will now begin to recuperate and will
begin to go from strength to strength. Should you need
to hire the talents and skills of other people, then this is
an ideal couple of days as you will certainly be getting
good value for money and will be pleased with the
work that is undertaken on your behalf. It is also a
time when, if you are single, you may meet someone
rather special.

JUNE

This month Uranus will be moving backwards into
your sign, increasing your willpower, independence,
originality, impulsiveness, liveliness, magnetism and
unconventionality. This is very much a time for pushing
ahead with all your ideas. Certainly on a financial level
you could be gaining in a rather unusual and even
complicated way. Don't be too quick then to brush
aside the eccentric ideas of other people, for when you
think about them at a later date you may realize that
they are not only viable but also highly profitable.

This month the Sun will be in the sign of Gemini
up until the 22nd. This is a great time for those of
you who work in the medical profession, for charities

or in the service industries. For all goats, this is a time when you will derive a great deal of pride from your achievements. You will be experiencing a warm inner glow in this direction. You are also more than ready to serve and help other people whenever you can, and just for once you will not insist on being 'top dog'. Your ability to be helpful and work alongside other people is certainly on the increase.

Mercury is in Gemini during June and resumes direct movement after the 17th, therefore put off signing documents or making important decisions until this date. The position of this planet in your chart will be encouraging a love of change and intellectual pursuits, such as chess. Furthermore you will see fascinating potential in everybody you meet. If you are a parent, you will be pleased with your offspring's progress and may be rewarding them for some achievement. You will also be forming many platonic relationships at this time. This is not to say that you will not have your share of emotional and sexual action. Far from it, and when Venus enters Taurus on 11 June you will be enjoying life to the fullest extent. Love affairs will develop so suddenly that you could be positively swept off your feet. However, you would be ill-advised to make any commitments for the time being as you and that other person are in a flirtatious mood. Socially, any entertainments which are arranged will go well. You are certainly playing the social butterfly.

It is a good time too for those involved in entertainment, the arts and sports. No matter where your main ambitions may lie, whether professional or emotional, this is a good time for attempting to make them come true because you are at your most approachable, easy-going and persuasive. Avoid the company of 'wet-blankets', and don't allow anybody to dampen your enthusiasm for life. Make up your mind what you want and then go after it. This is definitely a case of he who hesitates is lost.

Mars' placing in Virgo during June suggests that although you are in a charming and approachable mood, this does not mean that you do not have an iron will. Right now you are independent of thought and are prepared to fight for your convictions, no matter what. There will also be a tendency for you to love change, perhaps for the sake of it. This is all very uncharacteristic, but you should make the most of it while it lasts.

Now let us take a look at the state of the Moon. The full Moon this month occurs in the sign of Sagittarius on the 13th. Capricorn, like Cancer, can suffer from feelings of neglect and insecurity under the effects of a full Moon. However, provided you keep yourself busy and seek out congenial company, then this is easy to avoid. Be sure that you mix with friends who can bring a smile to your face or provide a willing ear to talk to.

Full Moons can be used constructively too, for they are useful for bringing projects or small phases of life to an end, particularly if they have proven to be non-productive. Use your full Moon period well and you need not waste even an hour feeling down in the mouth.

The new Moon this month occurs in the sign of Cancer on 28 June. This will be providing a boost to existing relationships and, if you are totally unattached, the possibility of meeting new people. There are likely to be several opportunities for you to become involved with the opposite sex and your popularity is certainly not in question. You are more responsive to the ideas, thoughts and feelings of other people at this time and your thoughtfulness will bring its own rewards. As ever, new Moons can be used effectively in the bringing about of change wherever you deem it is needed.

JULY

With no less than three planets in your opposite sign of Cancer, namely the Sun, Mercury and Venus, clearly the emphasis is on your closest relationships. You will be taking a certain pride in the way you are co-operating with other people, although it has to be said that you could be playing something of an opportunist, particularly where work matters are concerned. But why not – all is fair in love and work. Partnerships formed at the moment, whether professional or personal, are likely to be beneficial and it looks as if you are going to be making some ambitious plans in conjunction with somebody else.

This is the time of the year when you will be drawn to those who have a great deal in common with you on an intellectual level. Therefore you will be sharing your interests with like-minded people. Furthermore you will be much more affectionate in your approach to others and because of this will be able to pacify rivals and enemies. Few can resist you at the moment, Capricorn, therefore it is essential that you do not waste this period.

This is an especially good time for those of you who work on behalf of other people, such as agents or managers. Generally speaking, you are something of a lone wolf, but right now you understand the value of contacts and co-operation. This coming-together between yourself and other people not only works on a professional level but also on a personal level. Problems which may have been dogging a long-term relationship can be dealt with swiftly and you can get back on course far more quickly than you would have thought possible.

If you are fancy-free, this is not a time to play the recluse. Accept all invitations for socializing, get out and have fun, otherwise you could be seriously missing out.

Many of you will be meeting that special someone and those who have already given their heart away could be naming the day.

Financially, there is a suggestion that you could gain from signing a contract or perhaps going on some kind of professional trip. This is a great month too for facing up to the financial facts of life and planning your future.

Socially it is difficult to imagine you spending any time alone whatsoever, neither will you want to. You are surrounded by happy, humorous people, and are enjoying your life to the fullest extent.

Healthwise, it is hardly surprising that as the month wears on you could suffer from exhaustion. In order to avoid this, try to pace yourself a little more during the early part of the month and you will be able to keep going right through until the bitter end. Over-indulgence will be a strong temptation and one that for most of the time you won't bother to fight. However, too much eating, drinking and making merry could leave you a little jaded by the time this month is through and perhaps it might be a good idea to make some effort at being moderate.

Mars will be entering the sign of Libra at the zenith of your chart on 21 July. After this date the balance of your life will slowly shift towards professional matters, where you will have inexhaustible energy. However, do not attempt to take on too much. Where work is concerned, you are resolute, independent and are likely to find success through enterprise. This is a time when you will be sweeping all before you. For once you are living in the present and not twenty years ago or twenty years in the future.

Healthwise, increased workload is likely to find you feeling a little jaded at the end of the month, but it is the kind of happy exhaustion which you welcome, as you will certainly be feeling that you have made the most of your time – and you will be right.

Financially, because of the retrograde movement of Uranus, you would be ill-advised to spend without thought for the future. Clearly with such a sociable month ahead of you, you cannot avoid spending, but do not justify this by feeling you must impress other people. When are you going to learn, Capricorn, that all you need to be is yourself? That should be sufficient, and quite frankly if it isn't, then the other person isn't worth even considering.

All in all then, this is a month for you to jump feet first into life and squeeze as much as you can out of it.

Now let us look at the state of the Moon. A full Moon occurs in the sign of Capricorn on 12 July. Where one relationship is concerned, it is clearly a case of 'off with the old and on with the new'. You may also discover that you have a secret admirer as there will be a tendency for other people's emotions to rise to the surface and suddenly take you by surprise. Also, as usual, the full Moon can be used for putting the finishing touches to jobs and ideas, although it is not a good idea to start anything fresh at this time.

The new Moon during July occurs on the 27th in the sign of Leo. Regardless of your own sex, it is the females you know who are likely to be important around this time. Good news may be had in connection with a relative who has perhaps been feeling below par of late. Now, however, they will seem to be improving at an impressive rate. This is a good time too for meetings with bank managers and those in positions of power or authority. As always, the new Moon should be used for making fresh starts, so do not make this one an exception. All in all, July seems to be an extremely kind month to you. Be sure that you give it a helping hand and you won't regret it.

AUGUST

This month the Sun is in the sign of Leo up until 24
August. This is a time when you will be aware of
higher forces and will be intent on self-improvement.
You may also recruit the support of other people in
order to help you on a professional level. The current
position of the Sun suggests that you may be trying to
decide whether you wish to continue with an existing
relationship and much soul-searching seems to be going
on. However, you must weigh up the pros and the cons
dispassionately, and once you have made your decision,
stick to it no matter what.

This is an especially good time for those of you who
work in big institutions such as insurance, banking or
the stock exchange. It is also great for others who need
to deal with such people. Mercury moves into Virgo on
10 August and stays there for most of the month. This
will increase your mental inspiration and will help your
mind to be more flexible and adaptable. There may also
be a chance for you to travel, and if it should crop up
then do not hesitate to accept.

There will be times when you will behave in a
mercenary fashion, speedily making connections with
those who can help you out or help you up. Clearly the
business side to your sign is most active at the moment,
and will certainly be contributing to your success.

Mars continues at the zenith of your chart for this
entire period, and your workload seems to be extra
heavy. However, providing you can pace yourself or
even delegate, there is no reason why you should
become too exhausted.

Now is the time to remind you of one of the lessons
1995 is attempting to teach you. You have learned how
to come to terms with your immediate environment and
have chosen to identify yourself with one particular part

of it. Matters related to property, home and family all seem to be running well and you are feeling more secure than you have for some time. Now it is time to project yourself both at work and in the local community. During the remainder of the year, fight to increase your status and your efforts will not go to waste. There may also be an emphasis on the parent who had the most influence on you as you were growing up.

Healthwise, the only danger to you seems to come through overwork, but this is not unusual for you. Be sensible in this area and you should remain fit and healthy.

Fortunately Pluto resumes forward motion this month, therefore if you have suffered recently from disagreements with contacts, acquaintances and friends, now is the time for extending the olive branch and getting together with them once more. It is likely that both of you will have learned a lesson from this estrangement and your relationship will be all the stronger.

Jupiter too resumes forward motion during August. This will give you the valuable ability to win over opposition and enemies, and will also sharpen your instincts which you should listen to at all costs. Certainly you must use that practical and clever head, but do not forget to listen to that 'gut reaction' too. In this way you will be covering yourself in all areas.

Now let us look at the state of the Moon. The full Moon this month occurs in the sign of Aquarius on 10 August. A little bit of caution where finance is concerned is recommended during this period. For some reason there may be expenses and a rapid turnover. You will alternate between being careless and thrifty. Take care with your possessions too at this time as you could mislay something of a material or sentimental value.

The new Moon occurs in the sign of Virgo on 26 August. For many of you there may be an opportunity to travel or undertake a fresh course of learning. Others of you may decide it is time to change your image and a new, brighter and more confident you is likely to emerge. Your mind will be receptive and imaginative, and therefore it is an excellent time for the creative goat. As always, new Moons can be used for making fresh starts and adopting new ways of living. Ensure that you do not allow this period to go to waste. All in all, you have lots to look forward to in August.

SEPTEMBER

The Sun is in Virgo until 24 September and because of this you are likely to be at your most idealistic. You seem to be wiser too and will be handing on your experience to other people. Any chances to travel or to make contact with people from overseas should be snapped up as they will be lucky for you. It is certainly a good time for those of you in occupations connected with teaching, travel or foreign affairs. Your interest in your work and also in your social life is expanding. Be ready to accept new faces, places and ideas. Just when other people are beginning to think you are something of a stick-in-the-mud, you suddenly surprise them and are delighted at their reactions.

This can also be a profitable time for those of you dealing with legal matters, whether on a professional basis or by being involved in any kind of litigation. You should not allow yourself to be intimidated by anyone if you feel you are in the right.

During the first two weeks of this month, Venus is in Virgo, making you more sympathetic, understanding, intuitive, pleasant and positively inspired creatively. If you can use these characteristics in your work, you will certainly be doing well. If you are fancy-free, you may experience a mad, crazy attraction to someone from a totally different background to yourself. It is best not to make commitments for some while yet. Wait and see how things develop.

From 16 September onwards, Venus will be moving into Libra which is at the zenith of your chart and the area devoted to work. You will be mixing business with pleasure whenever possible and this could in turn lead to romance. Pleasant experiences are shown in connection with your professional life and the success could be gained through help from females where work is concerned.

Should it become necessary for you to sign any kind of document or travel for professional reasons, try to do so before 22 September when Mercury will resume retrograde action. This means that from our position in space, it will appear to be going backwards. When this occurs, untold chaos can happen where paperwork, documents and travelling are concerned. Don't take the risk, just be a little careful. Minor changes may also be going on in your place of employment and initially these may make you feel insecure. However, drag out your confidence and dust it down. This will enable you to keep things in their proper perspective.

Mars continues in Libra up until 7 September, therefore the first week of the month is likely to be the most hectic where professional matters are concerned. You possess inexhaustible energy and may attempt too much. Fiercely independent, you will resist any offers of help from other people. This, however, is most unwise. Take care you do not over-stretch yourself during this short period or you may damage other areas of your life for the remainder of the month.

Once Mars moves into Scorpio on 7 September, you will be developing some strong desires and powerful wishes. Socially, you will be playing the dominant role and making most of the decisions. It is likely too that you will be making many casual associations, perhaps of a physical nature. You will be drawn to energetic and enterprising people, although whether you will be able to keep up with them is open to question. Much depends on how much you are able to pace yourself earlier in the month – it is up to you.

Financially, now that Uranus has resumed forward movement, you begin to lose that feeling of 'two steps forward and three backwards'. Matters in this area slowly become less complicated and you begin to feel much more secure than you have done for some time.

Healthwise, apart from the danger of stress through overwork during the first week, you remain in good health and should be enjoying a lucky September.

Now let us look at the state of the Moon. The full Moon this month occurs in Pisces on the 9th. Around this time you may be a little imaginative, dreamy and even moody. This is a time then for keeping yourself busy from morning to night. Find something stimulating on which to work or keep company with the more active people of your circle. As usual, this is an ideal time for bringing matters to a head or clearing out the dead wood from your life, preparing to start again in the near future.

The new Moon this month occurs in the sign of Virgo on 24 September. This may be a time when you will change your opinions several times before coming down firmly on one side or the other. Certainly your mind is more imaginative and receptive which is good news if you are at all creative. It is also a good time for beginning a fresh line of study and planning a trip for the near future. All new beginnings made around this time in any area of life are certainly well starred.

OCTOBER

Now that Uranus and Neptune have resumed forward movement in your sign, you have increased magnetism, are strong willed, even more independent than usual, original, freedom-loving, unconventional and sensuous. Not surprisingly other people may be puzzled by your moods and behaviour on occasions, but they will also be strongly attracted to you.

This is a time of the year when a good deal of your energy – although by no means all of it – will be channelled into professional matters. You are determined to achieve success and a high position, and are strongly self-conscious too. The position of Mercury suggests that you are using your knowledge profitably and your adaptability will aid your career in some way. Minor changes at work can be implemented successfully. This is an especially happy time for those of you who are in positions of power or influence, involved with the commercial world, the literary world, travel or foreign affairs. Many of you will want to make minor changes to your ambitions and you should proceed in the confident knowledge that you are the only one who knows what is best for you – well, at this moment in time anyway. However, with so much energy being channelled into professional matters, you must be sure that you do not neglect loved ones or the family, otherwise there could be some loud protests.

Romantically, during the first ten days of October, the position of Venus in Libra suggests that romance could very well enter your life through professional matters. Certainly chances to mix business with pleasure will be frequent. Pleasant experiences will occur because of this and you will meet several people with whom you may consider starting a relationship. From 10 October onwards, Venus will be entering the sign of Scorpio, so for the rest of the month you will be fond of company and will be more affectionate and find happiness and stimulation through artistic and cultured friends. Should you be fancy-free, it is unlikely that you will seriously consider making a commitment. You seem to be having far too much fun for that at the moment.

Regardless of your sex, it is the females in your circle who will play a guiding role in your life during October and their influence will be beneficial. Mars will be moving into Sagittarius on 21 October, and once this occurs you will be able to turn anything that happens to you to your advantage. However, be warned that you are strongly impulsive at this time and you should think carefully before making promises that you may not be able to keep in the future.

Financially, money is being spent on socializing, although you are in a practical mood and will not spend more than you can afford.

Healthwise, it is possible that you will tire easily during the first fourteen days of the month, but providing you can get in at least one early night you should survive intact. Following this date, over-indulgence seems to be your only problem, but this is not really a problem to you. The goat invariably manages to eat or drink anything without much effect, and providing this doesn't go on for too long, then no harm will be done.

Now let us look at the state of the Moon. The full Moon this month occurs in the sign of Aries on 8 October. Around this time, you will feel an inner desire for peace and security. You may even insulate yourself against the rest of the world by withdrawing for the day. This is certainly not a time for confrontations or making decisions.

The new Moon this month occurs in the sign of Scorpio on 24 October, making this a period when you

will be at your most popular. You will be making social
contact and forming many new acquaintances. Should
there be any misunderstandings between yourself, contacts or friends, now is the time for clearing them up.
As usual, new Moons can be used for making fresh
starts in any area of life. Therefore do not hesitate to
implement plans that you have been thinking about for
some while.

NOVEMBER

During the first three weeks of this month, the Sun will
be joining Mercury in the sign of Scorpio. This will be
making you socially ambitious and will increase your
ability to co-operate with other people more successfully. Your popularity will not be in question and you
will be making firm, faithful and influential friends.
Your mind will be more active and quicker at picking
up new techniques and ideas. You will be attracted
to intellectual and adaptable people and will prefer to
spend your time with new faces rather than with the
same old crowd. Because of this, it is highly likely that
you may be developing a new ambition in life.

November is certainly a profitable and lucky time for
those of you who work as a member of a team, whether
professionally or socially, and is also a good time for
dealing with administration in its many guises.

Financially, there will be chances for you to swell your
bank account on various occasions. For these you should
refer to the day-to-day guide.

Throughout November, there are no less than four
planets wending their way through the sign of Sagittarius.
Mars will be helping you to turn matters to your own
advantage, although it could be suppressing your sexual
desires. The reason for this may be traced to the position

of Venus in the same area which suggests that you are
more than usually sensitive and selfish. There is also a
chance that you may be attracted to the wrong people.
Where emotions and sex are concerned, you could very
well be your own worst enemy in some way. Naturally
the stars impel, but they do not compel, therefore this
statement is not providing you with an excuse to behave
outrageously. Rather it is a warning about what can
occur if you are not a little more scrupulous about the
company you keep.

Certainly those of you already in a steady relationship
may for one reason or another feel unable to express
yourself openly at the moment. Possibly your partner
may have wittingly or unwittingly hurt you. Should the
latter apply, you can hardly expect them to understand
what is going on. Therefore, Capricorn, do not withdraw
so far into yourself that you are totally lost to the outside
world. If you have a grievance of a personal nature, then
wait for the appropriate moment, sit that other person
down and talk things through. Avoid recrimination and
nagging which will get you precious little in the way of
progress. A sensible discussion followed by a kiss and
a cuddle will serve you a great deal better.

Friends seem to play a large part in the major events
of the month. They will be inviting you to join them on
many occasions and you should accept any invitation
you can. Club activities are especially well starred,
especially if you participate in any kind of team sport.
Debating groups will be stimulating and acquaintances
and contacts will become fast friends overnight. This is
one of the most sociable times of the year, and although
you are enjoying yourself simply for the sake of letting
off steam, it is also likely that ulterior motives are at
work here. Let's face it, you can play the opportunist
when the need arises, as it could very well do during
November.

Should there be any Sagittarians in your family or in your cluster of friends, then they are likely to be exercising a tremendous amount of influence over you throughout this month. Now, Capricorn, you can learn a lot from this sign as there is nobody like a Sagittarian to provide humour and a light-hearted atmosphere, and generally to chase away everybody's blues. In fact, if you can learn to be as light-hearted as this sign, you will be doing yourself a big favour.

Where love and sex are concerned, this month you are advised to continue to play the field if you are fancy-free. You will behave like a child in a sweet shop with so many opportunities you won't know which way to turn. Take each day as it comes and worry about heavy commitment another time. Should you already be in a relationship, it is likely that you will be spending precious little time with your partner, unless of course you can persuade them to join you in the many activities you are involved with at this time.

Healthwise, aside from feeling a little jaded from the intense activity in your social life, you seem to manage quite comfortably to work during the day and play most of the night. However, out of respect for your own physical wellbeing you should get in at least one or two early nights.

Needless to say, with such a heavy schedule it is unlikely you will have time to dwell on past failures. For the most part you will be in a positive mood and ready to accept life's challenges and opportunities.

Now let's look at the state of the Moon. The full Moon falls in the sign of Taurus on 7 November, suggesting that if you are a parent you may have a decision to make on behalf of your offspring. If not, then a chance to become involved with an artistic project may crop up, although you will be unable to do so until you have finished existing projects. As always, full Moons are a great time for bringing a set of circumstances to an end.

The new Moon will fall in the sign of Scorpio on 22 November, throwing the emphasis yet again on to the friendship and contact area of life. New people who enter your life at this time could prove to be most useful in professional matters. Alternatively, they could come to mean a great deal to you on an emotional level in the not too distant future.

On no account allow yourself to feel guilty simply because you are devoting so much of your time to sheer enjoyment. After all, you are one of the plough horses of the zodiac and no doubt you can catch up with anything that has been left unfinished in the near future. In the meantime, have fun.

DECEMBER

December is a month that bodes well for those who work behind the scenes, such as in research, science or the medical profession, or as a wardrobe mistress, hairdresser etc. This is a much quieter month, but you will probably welcome this as you have been rushed off your feet recently. Despite this, there will be a tendency for you to withdraw into one of your antisocial moods. You may justify this by telling yourself that of late you have been playing the social butterfly and now is the time to 'bring up the drawbridge'. Certainly there is something in this, but is it really necessary for a whole month? I think this may be taking things a little too far! If necessary, you must force yourself out into life as there are opportunities out there which you will not wish to miss out on.

Nevertheless, you are at your most sensitive and aware of undercurrents and atmospheres both between

people and in environments. Should you use your
intuition on a professional level, this will certainly be
a profitable and enjoyable month. Luckily Venus will
be in your sign up until 22 December. This planet of
love, creativity and socializing will not allow you to hide
away from the world for too long. You will be at your
most affectionate, harmony-seeking and sympathetic,
but will also be in strong need of some appreciation.
It is obvious that your vulnerability could prove to be
irresistible to the opposite sex and, providing you can
persuade yourself out into the world, it is quite likely
that you could meet someone special. Therefore I think
the effort could be well worthwhile.

Any relationships of a personal or professional nature
which are formed during December are likely to be
important for many years to come. Some of you may
even be planning a Christmas engagement; if so, you
have chosen well. Others need to be especially careful
when mixing business with pleasure as office or factory
romances could suddenly flare up. However, they are
sure to be short-lived.

Financially, you are more prepared to spend on luxu-
ries than usual and those who are closest to you are sure
to be spoiled by an overly generous mood.

Chances to have fun are certainly on the increase and
you must force yourself out into the world. If you do,
you will be glad you made the effort as the rest of the
world will be only too happy to welcome you into it.

Healthwise, despite activities which may be taking
their toll, you will manage to remain boisterous and
full of life for the majority of December, only flagging
on rare occasions.

This year is likely to end with some exciting news of
a financial nature and this will set you up for 1996 in
the best possible way.

All in all, by the time this year is through, you will

realize that you have made a great deal of steady progress and will be looking forward to even greater success during the year that lies ahead.

Now let us take a look at the state of the Moon. The full Moon this month occurs in the sign of Gemini on 7 December. Should you be attending any kind of get-together at this time, then you may find your stamina isn't quite up to its usual level of excellence and you may need to take your pleasures a little less enthusiastically. There may also be an opportunity for you to help a workmate. You are sure to pick up on it and will be earning some undying gratitude. However, this is a day when your partner could be acting out of character and it is up to you to find out why.

The new Moon occurs in the sign of Sagittarius on 22 December, making this a time when you will be discarding old habits and ideas. As a rule, you tend to adopt this attitude on New Year's Eve, but this year have decided on some radical changes and are beginning a little early. This is also a period when good ideas are forming in your head. You will be laying down some good constructive plans for the future which you will no doubt utilize as soon as the new year begins. Those closest to you on this day are at their most gregarious and adventurous. Like it or not, you will be dragged out kicking and screaming only to decide later that you were glad you went along with their suggestions. This is therefore a positive period with much to offer.

Daily Guide

JANUARY

SUNDAY 1st It's new Moon day and it falls in your sign, therefore no matter what cards you have been dealt recently you will now be in a position to play them to your advantage. This is also a time for ringing the changes, beginning anything new and generally stepping forward into the spotlight and drawing attention to yourself. Generally you prefer to wait in the wings, but now is the time to gather the recognition that is long overdue.

MONDAY 2nd This is one of the most important days of the month. The new Moon continuing in your sign signals the start of a new phase in your life. In order to make the most of it, however, you must first dispose of anything that is outdated. Soon you will be given the opportunity to settle a family or domestic dispute. Do whatever is necessary to make peace.

TUESDAY 3rd Do try to make the most of any time you have to yourself today because what you discover in contemplation will be of great value. This may be a quiet day, giving you time to evaluate what has taken place recently. There have been many changes and not all of them to your liking. Ask yourself what needs to be changed now to make your future more exciting.

WEDNESDAY 4th Like most people, you sometimes find it difficult to keep pace with your own ideas and also other people's. Today, the Moon in Aquarius means you now have a chance to realize some of your dreams. However, the more you try to find the answer to several problems at once, the less you will achieve. Therefore try to concentrate on what you see as the most pressing problems.

THURSDAY 5th There are clearly two personality types born under your sign, those who climb up the mountain a step at a time, and those who remain chained in the yard. However, you simply can't go wrong right now. Success might come with promotional pay rises in the near future. Of course, there is no such thing as something for nothing, so whatever you receive today will be richly deserved.

FRIDAY 6th The Moon in Pisces will give you the opportunity to put some of your dearest ideas into practice. How successful you are relies on you finding the correct balance between reality and theory. It's one thing to know what needs to be done, but quite another to find the right way of doing it. A little bit of thought will take you a long way.

SATURDAY 7th The planet of Mercury moves into the financial area of your life where it will stay for a couple of weeks. During this period you must not allow misunderstandings over money to make you feel insecure. Have faith in your own abilities and judgement as they are likely to be spot-on at this time. Paperwork will be important and it is an ideal time for signing contracts.

SUNDAY 8th Venus moves into Sagittarius today, the area of your chart devoted to hopes, wishes and dreams.

This is therefore a perfect time for assessing where you have come in life to date, and where you wish to be in the future. Think long and hard before committing yourself to changes in job, home or outlook, as you will need to bear the consequences for some time to come. Also avoid becoming involved with members of the opposite sex who are already spoken for.

MONDAY 9th This morning you simply do not have time to fit everything in which needs your attention, therefore slow down and spread your activities over the entire day instead of attempting to solve everything in a matter of hours. You have all the time in the world and as a goat you tend to do better when you are progressing at a steady trot rather than a mad sprint.

TUESDAY 10th Don't for one moment think that you can spend your way out of any kind of difficulty. What is needed now is not a fresh injection of cash, but a new approach to both professional and personal problems. You might even need to shut yourself away from outside influences and think again about the best way to proceed.

WEDNESDAY 11th Look to the future with confidence and a positive attitude today. Don't be afraid to press ahead with schemes or plans which have been under consideration for a while now. You must remember, however, to keep colleagues and loved ones informed of your moods and motives. You want to avoid any serious disagreement, and you can't afford to anger or antagonize the wrong people.

THURSDAY 12th Your long-term prospects get more promising by the day, but short-term problems continue. You possess many talents, and one of them is almost to make an art form of worrying! Regrettably you cannot push to one side what is bothering you as it keeps nagging away at the back of your mind. You will just have to confront those who have upset you, even at the risk of creating a scene.

FRIDAY 13th The Moon in Gemini suggests that at work it would be a good idea to attempt to force or persuade colleagues to confront matters they have been trying to avoid for some time now. They seem to be looking to you to solve a problem, but realistically you cannot take on board anything else for the time being. Try to persuade them to stand on their own two feet.

SATURDAY 14th There is a wonderful aspect between Jupiter, the planet of luck, and Venus which suggests you can find a perfect balance between financial and business matters right now. Life has not been easy in recent weeks, but your determination has not gone unnoticed by those who matter most, both at home and at work. In fact, your efforts over this time are about to be paid back in full – plus interest.

SUNDAY 15th Events which took place yesterday may have come as something of a surprise. As a result, you may find you neglect to take advantage of them. Whatever chances you are offered right now, don't think for a moment you have not earned them or do not deserve them. Use them, profit by them and, above all, enjoy them.

MONDAY 16th The full Moon in your opposite sign of Cancer will make you acutely aware of recent difficulties. It is possible that something or someone may have tied you to the past while a much brighter future beckons. Now you should begin to feel that everything you have endured has been worthwhile. The future certainly looks a good deal brighter.

TUESDAY 17th Do try to concentrate on what you do best. There are times when even down-to-earth Capricorn can be overwhelmed by the need to do something on impulse. This, however, would be completely the wrong way to travel today. There is pride and money at stake. Be sure that you do not live to regret hasty decisions.

WEDNESDAY 18th The Moon in Leo suggests that you are thinking long and hard about an official matter or possibly mulling over a contract, but if you are in any kind of doubt the best thing to do is to go to the experts. You may be a clever goat, but you cannot know everything about every subject in the book. Avoid any kind of bluff, it simply won't work at the moment. Proceed in your usual practical way, namely a step at a time.

THURSDAY 19th Pluto temporarily moves into the sign of Sagittarius, and although this could be stirring up all kinds of insecurities, you must continue to think as positively as possible. Bear in mind all that you have achieved in the last eighteen months or so, and resolve to continue to progress despite obstacles and the opinions of other people, both at work and at home. Strengthen your resolve and you really cannot go wrong.

FRIDAY 20th The Moon in Virgo makes this an ideal time for reaching out into life and making changes. If you have been considering learning a fresh skill or perhaps changing your image, then this is the ideal time for doing so. Those of you with friends or loved ones abroad are likely to be hearing from them.

SATURDAY 21st Today the Sun moves into the financial area of life and therefore your concentration will be strongly focused on money matters over the next couple of weeks. It is definitely an ideal time for those of you who work in finance or for goats who wish to talk over such matters with the so-called 'experts'. You will have a natural instinct to conserve as much as possible.

SUNDAY 22nd The Moon is in Libra, the zenith of your chart, and suggests that you keep as high a profile as is possible. Now is not the time to play the shrinking violet, but the bright and cheerful sunflower. Remember that you are as good, and perhaps even better, than other people, so do not allow them to drag you down or stress you out. This is a good time for mixing business with pleasure.

MONDAY 23rd Mars moves into retrograde movement today, and you could end up like a juggler with one too many balls in the air. Certainly you are sensible enough to be aware of your limitations, and emotionally, personally and professionally, balance counts for everything over the next couple of days. Without it, no amount of juggling will stop you making a fool of yourself.

TUESDAY 24th This is an ideal time for tying up loose ends and laying plans for the next couple of months. You could not wish for a luckier time for trying new jobs and setting new objectives for yourself. If you can dream about it, you can also do it. Keep faith with yourself and nothing will be impossible.

WEDNESDAY 25th The Moon in Scorpio today suggests that no matter how many times you may have knocked on one door in vain, you should try again. In fact, the aspects today suggest that all you have to do in order to get the right answers is to ask the right questions. This is a time when you should decide to boost your reputation and stabilize your finances.

THURSDAY 26th Today, Mercury moves into retrograde action, and therefore it is best during the next couple of weeks to avoid signing contracts. If it is necessary to travel, then for heaven's sake double-check all of your details as something will go awry and waste your time. Also avoid making unnecessary changes until Mercury resumes forward action.

FRIDAY 27th The Moon in Sagittarius suggests that you must try to strike the right balance between your spiritual and material needs. Above all else, don't allow others' behaviour or financial problems to undermine you. In fact, take note of what occurs today because the same situation may recur next month. Remember that no life is so difficult that it can't be made easier by the way you lead it.

SATURDAY 28th The Moon in your sign suggests that tensions that have been simmering beneath the surface for quite some time now are ready to burst into the open. At least one important personal or professional relationship may never be the same. Soon the stars will be giving you the green light to make changes, not only of emphasis but also of scene.

SUNDAY 29th You express strong likes and dislikes, and there is nothing you dislike more than unexpected change. This is why you really must take advantage of today in order to overhaul your working pattern on your own terms. Otherwise, what seems to be a good opportunity may turn out to be a distinct disadvantage.

MONDAY 30th The new Moon in Aquarius today will be providing you with an ideal chance to prove your worth, particularly where a financial matter is concerned. There may also be a fresh source of income for you to consider. Take a couple of days before coming down on one side or the other. This is a great time for beginning anything new.

TUESDAY 31st You can find success keeping long-term goals in mind while concentrating on the job in hand. Something may occur today which will make it abundantly clear that you are heading in the right direction as far as property, family and financial matters are concerned. In fact, your determination and confidence should be soaring.

FEBRUARY

WEDNESDAY 1st Although you would never intentionally say anything to hurt partners or workmates, neither are you the type to hold back, and as the Moon is active in the communication section of your chart, there may be times when you say more than is wise. Your words could return to haunt you, so where necessary make amends and apologize. An error acknowledged is a victory won.

THURSDAY 2nd One of the rules of life is that we gain from it in direct proportion to what we put in. So don't think twice before accepting what is on offer today, even if you believe others deserve it more. Part of your problem is that you are too modest. This constantly holds you back and leads to less talented people making off with all the glory which should be yours. Expect less today and you will get it.

FRIDAY 3rd Today you really won't mind if other people walk in front of you. Despite this, you will still manage to be the one that gets to the top first. But does the road wind uphill all of the way, and will anyone ever appreciate just how sensitive, soft and emotionally vulnerable you really are? These are questions you will be asking yourself today.

SATURDAY 4th The Sun is in a beautiful aspect with quicksilver Mercury in the financial area of life. Therefore you could be picking up bargains and be more prone to brilliant money-making schemes. Should the latter apply, then get out a pen and pad before your ideas completely disappear out of your head. If you are out shopping today, you are bound to be picking up bargains and meeting interesting new people.

SUNDAY 5th Today Venus moves into your sign, encouraging you to turn your attention to romantic and social matters over the next couple of weeks. Those of you in steady relationships may finally decide to name the day. For others, there may be an interesting and profitable professional partnership which is formed.

MONDAY 6th Mercury lines up with lucky Jupiter in the financial area of life, therefore you can expect an opportunity to come your way where a contract is concerned. Should it be necessary for you to sign a contract, try to procrastinate until after 17 February when Mercury resumes forward action. After this you get the green light from the stars.

TUESDAY 7th   There are Capricorns who are wildly romantic and impulsive, and this is certainly true while the Moon is in the sign of Taurus. However, the bottom line is that life is a serious business for those born under the sign of the goat. 'Wouldn't it be fantastic if . . .?' and 'I should have . . .' – don't these two statements sound familiar? They certainly will today.

WEDNESDAY 8th   Just like yesterday, there is a certain amount of wishful thinking going on, and this is likely to be due to the fact that you are avoiding the truth concerning a situation. The reality of the matter is that your chart at the moment is confused and uncertain. In fact, you appear to be recovering from surprises which occurred a couple of weeks ago. Take some time before making emotional commitments.

THURSDAY 9th   You generally manage to come up like new, and no matter how strong the opposition is, you alway win through. Today it could be different. The fiery planet Mars is in retrograde action, consequently there seem to be movements which you can't explain or situations which can't be handled in the usual manner.

FRIDAY 10th   The only way to proceed today is to relax your efforts and wait and see what occurs after the full Moon. This may bring certain things to light. Remember that looking at small advantages often prevents greater things from being accomplished.

SATURDAY 11th   Although Capricorn is ruled by sensible Saturn, the planet of ambition, achievement and recognition, nevertheless you appear to have experienced difficulty recently in communicating your thoughts on these particular subjects. You are likely to astound everyone now by your ability to communicate, your enthusiasm and your self-confidence.

SUNDAY 12th The Moon in your opposite sign of Cancer will certainly be making those closest to you changeable, emotional and sentimental. You are a practical soul and may have little patience with this, but you must remember that relationships involve both give and take and it is now your turn to do the giving. New people you meet today will certainly illuminate your life for some time to come.

MONDAY 13th The Moon's position in Leo in the next couple of days finds you indecisive about a current relationship. You are not sure whether you wish to continue it any longer, but if you agree to do so, then you must accept the fact that people do not change, no matter how hard you may wish them to. After all, even you would find it difficult to step outside your basic personality.

TUESDAY 14th This is a particularly good time for those of you involved in banking, the stock exchange or big business. It is also good for other goats who wish to deal with such people. In these areas you can afford to push ahead with confidence in the knowledge that right is on your side. Do not allow yourself to be intimidated by anyone.

WEDNESDAY 15th The full Moon today could spring a few surprises in your intimate circle of friends, as well as among your loved ones. Other people are acting out of character and you find it difficult to keep pace with their thoughts and action. Avoid applying any kind of pressure or somebody could exit permanently from your life and you may not be able to undo this state of affairs.

THURSDAY 16th The Moon in Virgo makes this an ideal time for dealing with legal matters, foreign affairs or long distance travel. It is a good time too for those whose work depends on inspiration and creativity – in this area you are unbeatable and should push ahead of rivals and competitors. This evening you will need stimulating company.

FRIDAY 17th Venus lines up with your ruling planet Saturn, and because of this it is time to reap the rewards of work done many moons ago. Before this day is over you are sure to have reasons for celebration. A serious attitude to your emotions is also expected.

SATURDAY 18th Mercury finally resumes direct movement and now you can push ahead with travel matters, paperwork and documents. Legal affairs can also be given a hearty shove, and if you need a time for settling out of court in the next couple of weeks this is an ideal time to do so.

SUNDAY 19th Today the Sun moves into the communication section of your chart in the sign of Pisces. You will therefore find it a great deal easier to express yourself, both emotionally as well as mentally. Chances to pay visits, whether on a professional or personal level, should be snapped up. The affairs of a brother or sister are also likely to be highlighted during the next month.

MONDAY 20th A major career or professional change is certainly suggested, even though the actual move itself cannot be put into operation until later in the year. No doubt there will be the odd moment when you feel uncertain and out of sorts, but on no account allow self-doubt, or worse, self-pity, to creep in.

TUESDAY 21st   With the Moon in the sign of Scorpio, you can expect those closest to you to be more intense, passionate and dogmatic than usual. This is an ideal time for developing flexibility. There is plenty of news in connection with friends, and you socialize far more than usual.

WEDNESDAY 22nd   Now the Moon has entered into the sign of Sagittarius, you are provided with a couple of days in which to deliberate and decide what your next move should be. On no account rush into relationships or situations before giving them due thought.

THURSDAY 23rd   This is an ideal day for looking behind the scenes in order to uncover facts and situations which seem to be shrouded in mystery. With your determination, it should be relatively easy for you to throw the spotlight of truth and illumination on to anything or anyone which is in the slightest bit complicated, uncertain or even devious.

FRIDAY 24th   The Moon in your sign suggests that you are likely to be responding to practical issues from an emotional standpoint. Try to keep a sensible head on your shoulders at all times, especially if you have important decisions to make. Luckily though, this aspect is sure to benefit the personal side of your life where you will be adopting a softer approach.

SATURDAY 25th   While the Moon is in contact with Uranus and Neptune as it is today, there is a risk of matrimonial or partnership problems – and of your spending too much time worrying about your failings. It is therefore important that you turn your attention to external matters in order to overcome these problems. They can be settled at a later date.

SUNDAY 26th Venus and Neptune suggest that you will come to realize that there is more to having a job then simply showing up for work. In other words, if you are at present dissatisfied with your working routine, a series of events will afford you the chance to air your frustrations and grievances and you should not hesitate to do so. However, romance is extremely well starred.

MONDAY 27th Like the other earth signs, Taurus and Virgo, the problem with your sign is stubbornness, so breaking the habit of a lifetime won't be easy. However, if you are ready to listen and watch what is going on around you, then you will know precisely what action needs to be taken. Problems are frequently the price to be paid for progress and opportunity, although this is sometimes hard to recognize if one is simply looking for a lucky break.

TUESDAY 28th Venus is in beautiful aspect to your financial planet, Uranus, and you must be quick to snap up all opportunities to step into the future with greater self-confidence and the knowledge that you are on the right track. There is an unexpected feel about romance which could be exciting.

MARCH

WEDNESDAY 1st Today is a new Moon day and it occurs in the sign of Pisces. Just for once, why not let the planets determine your future role? The storms which have made strife in partnerships and emotional turbulence difficult to bear now begin to abate and you will see the future clearly signposted. In fact, rarely have you been in such a strong position to make your mark.

THURSDAY 2nd Sometimes your own difficulties seem so overwhelming you give little thought to other people's dilemmas or lives. When this occurs, you lack the ability to be sympathetic and warm-hearted and this is certainly a pitfall you need to watch out for today. The Moon in Pisces right now will be making those closest to you at their most vulnerable and it is up to you to respond in the correct way.

FRIDAY 3rd Today Venus moves into the financial area of life. Therefore you must now concentrate on recouping all that is owed to you and paying out what is due to other people. Should you be experiencing any kind of difficulties, you may find females extremely useful when it comes to handing out advice. It is likely that somebody will be speaking to you from a position of vast experience.

SATURDAY 4th Pluto moves into retrograde action today, and you are likely to be on your own when it comes to making world-shattering decisions, as friends, contacts and acquaintances are either too busy or too preoccupied with their own life to lend a helping hand. Never mind, you are one of the most independent signs in the zodiac.

SUNDAY 5th The Moon in Taurus will be encouraging all the pleasure-loving sides to your character. Now is the time for making arrangements to let off steam and allow the cares of recent months to drift away, if only for a couple of days. Romance is likely to be fun and flirtatious too.

MONDAY 6th The Moon in Taurus will be lending a helping hand to those of you in creative or sporty jobs. Last minute adjustments to plans should be made before putting them into operation. Those of you waiting on news from loved ones should not be disappointed.

TUESDAY 7th There are times when you can be soft, gentle and compassionate, and this is one of them. Compassion is a virtue which suggests you have room in your heart for other people. Right now you are able to offer a haven where others can find safety and security. This is also a good time for parents who wish to make changes on behalf of their children.

WEDNESDAY 8th The combination of sexy Mars with lucky Jupiter in a sensitive part of your chart will coincide with meeting exciting and stimulating companions or even a new love affair. Domestic instincts will be strong and it is the ideal time for putting relationships on a more secure footing.

THURSDAY 9th Mars continues to line up with Jupiter and this will be providing many opportunities for you to grow and expand in life. There is an especially lucky glow over property and family matters and any long-standing problems in these areas can be solved. This is a great time for entertaining at home.

FRIDAY 10th Where professional matters are concerned, you must ensure that you have all the essential figures and facts regarding one particular project. The indecision of a workmate or an employer could cause you some embarrassment. As a Capricorn, you demand unswerving loyalty from those closest to you and you should now be reorganizing your life for greater security and stability in a new environment.

SATURDAY 11th A recent combination of Mars with lucky Jupiter in the sensitive area of your chart has probably coincided with excitement, stimulating companionship or even a new love affair. Your domestic impulses are likely to be strengthened and it is an ideal time for putting relationships on a more secure footing. Always remember that provided you are prepared to go to any length to preserve and protect all that is precious to you, you can weather any storms and emerge victorious.

SUNDAY 12th   With the Moon in Cancer, it would be wise to go along with the ideas and plans of other people today. Do not insist on always having your own way, and remember that by giving you are in fact receiving. New people who enter your life right now will be important for quite some time. It is a newsy as well as an active day.

MONDAY 13th   Although it is true that a workmate or colleague may owe you a great deal in return for your support, it is probably not the appropriate time to call in this debt, for in doing so a misunderstanding could result. It is far better to allow others to come to the realization on their own. If they refuse to do so, you can always withdraw any further help.

TUESDAY 14th   Long-standing disagreements must be settled if you are to protect your long-term security. This may mean coming to your senses and not allowing emotions to influence your judgement. Luckily you have a wise and sympathetic contact who realizes this is a most decisive and important phase workwise, and you now need a great deal of support if you are to emerge triumphant.

WEDNESDAY 15th   That planet of love and creativity, Venus, is now lining up with lucky, expansive Jupiter.

This is therefore a time when you should allow your heart to rule that businesslike head, and at all costs avoid taking your work problems back home to your partner. It looks as though you may have been neglecting your mate for some time now and this will be the ideal time for making recompense.

THURSDAY 16th Today Mercury moves into the communications area of your chart. The emphasis is going to be on short trips and travel during the next few weeks. Those of you attending meetings and negotiations are sure to shine. You must push ahead with confidence and allow your belief in yourself to shine through your eyes.

FRIDAY 17th Today the full Moon in the sign of Virgo could make long distance travelling complicated. If it is necessary for you to set out on a trip, you should double-check all arrangements, particularly paperwork. News from abroad is likely to be delayed and this could cause frustration.

SATURDAY 18th The Moon at the zenith of your chart advises you to keep a high profile today. Generally you work away in the background, trying to do the best you can for your loved ones without expecting any kind of reward or recognition. However, if you continue in this way, you may find you are being taken for granted, and this will never do.

SUNDAY 19th Later today the Moon moves into Scorpio, the friendship and contact area of life. This is a great day for visiting any kind of club and making new friends. Any advice that you need is likely to be forthcoming from the older and more experienced members of your circle. Do not hesitate to approach them.

MONDAY 20th The Sun is in beautiful aspect to Uranus today which should certainly be providing a fillip to your finances. What's more, you must be ready to take advantage of the lively prevailing conditions and snap up all opportunities to do yourself a bit of good.

TUESDAY 21st The Sun is lining up with Pluto, and this strongly suggests that it is time to sweep away the dead wood from your life before proceeding any further. It is also a good time for discarding old habits and making changes of direction. Remember, nothing will ever stay the same – life is about movement.

WEDNESDAY 22nd Today the Moon occupies the sign of Sagittarius. This seems to suggest you have learned how to take setbacks in your stride, and although employers or colleagues will tax your patience, the best course of action is to say little and wait until later before you take appropriate action.

THURSDAY 23rd You seem to be coming to your senses as far as an emotional attachment is concerned and you are now able to tie up a number of loose ends and say goodbye to certain individuals without a trace of guilt or remorse. This will lead you to concentrate on people who have your best interests at heart.

FRIDAY 24th A confrontation with a workmate or loved one may become necessary today in order to get your point of view across. A more forceful and self-interested approach on your part is required. This may seem to you to be a little selfish, but you can no longer go on sacrificing yourself to others' wants and needs.

SATURDAY 25th Your ruling planet, Saturn, is beautifully aspected by communicative and quicksilver Mercury. The whole day is jam-packed with activity and most of it will be instigated by yourself. Your quick wits and ready laugh will make you most attractive to the opposite sex and this could be a memorable time for romance.

SUNDAY 26th Be sure that you do not overspend on entertainment today. There will be a strong temptation for you to do so. Also, hang on to possessions, particularly when you are in crowds as something could go missing, and you may waste a good deal of your valuable time looking for it.

MONDAY 27th You may be strongly tempted into extravagance today and you need all your steely willpower to avoid this. You have finally managed to overcome most of your financial problems, and the last thing you need to do is set yourself back by a foolish act of impulse. This is an excellent time for attending financial meetings. This evening get out and relax.

TUESDAY 28th The entrance of Venus into Pisces will certainly mark the beginning of a harmonious trend and will leave its signature on a close relationship or love affair. Professional matters and established business ties are also under harmonious influences, although something that has been simmering away in the background could erupt unexpectedly at a later date.

WEDNESDAY 29th It is likely that recently a relative has given you cause for worry, but luckily with your past

support they seem to be pulling through and you begin
to relax in this area. You may even decide to celebrate
in a minor way, and this will give you the opportunity
to relax and unwind a little.

THURSDAY 30th Mercury and Neptune are attempting to illuminate the way forward. Even so, do not be in
too much of a rush – you have some financial interests
which you must consolidate, rather than being tempted
to over-extend yourself. It is time really for putting the
finishing touches to jobs and situations before you
allow yourself to be tempted into fresh commitments
or challenges.

FRIDAY 31st The new Moon today falls in the family
and property area of life where there is a minor new
beginning. There will be some pleasant news in connection with a relative which will be putting your
mind at ease. Entertaining at home will be especially
enjoyable.

APRIL

SATURDAY 1st Although business and financial affairs
could be better, nevertheless there are plenty of compen-
sations in the form of a reasonably satisfying love life
and the much needed support of friends, particularly
today. Snap up any chances to take part in a sporting
occasion or go to a party where you can really relax.

SUNDAY 2nd Mercury lines up with Pluto and you
are likely to find friends and acquaintances in a changeable frame of mind. It is possible too that you may be
affected by sudden emergencies and they may find it
necessary to cancel arrangements with you. Do not take

this slight personally, as they have little choice in the matter.

MONDAY 3rd The Sun lines up with sexy, aggressive Mars today and this certainly will be providing you with a great deal of activity and opportunity. Changes can also be made at home where members of the family are anxious to do your bidding for a change. Property matters are also well starred.

TUESDAY 4th As an earth sign, your natural impulse is to express yourself cautiously and to make decisions based on thorough and practical assessment of situations, always taking into account every eventuality. This usually works splendidly, but today is a time for widening your experience and making bigger leaps, either emotionally or professionally.

WEDNESDAY 5th Because you are preoccupied with some kind of dispute, it is impossible to get a true perspective or to see it in its wider context. The chances are that you have already analysed the situation to a point where it has become meaningless. Now that benevolent Jupiter has joined forces with the Sun, you are at a delicate stage as far as negotiations are concerned. For the best results, postpone final decisions till a little later.

THURSDAY 6th There is an unpredictable quality to today, and you may find things don't go according to plan and you have to do a hasty rethink. However, with Jupiter continuing on your side, it will be a complete waste of time to worry about what has been.

FRIDAY 7th Today the stars indicate that you are not quite out of the woods as far as a delicate career issue is concerned. The situation seems threatening because you feel out of your depth, but you have more power to influence the outcome than you realize. If you recognize this and act appropriately, you can subsequently set a course of action into motion.

SATURDAY 8th There seems to be some kind of deadlock which is cropping up in your love life. You should talk about your problems and keep talking until your partner listens. Luckily, with the Moon in Cancer you will find them relatively receptive. This is an ideal time to put away differences which have been hanging around for far too long now. If you are single, you could meet somebody new and exciting.

SUNDAY 9th Mercury and Mars line up today, and this will certainly be enlivening matters at home. If you are entertaining there, you will be doing so with your usual style and aplomb and will impress other people. Children may be a little unruly, but you have enough energy and can cope well. Sporting events are also well starred, as is romance.

MONDAY 10th People you least expect to assist you could reappear. With their help you should find that you fall on your feet and are able to make an important decision involving a small risk. Creative and imaginative projects could prove to be the highlight of your day. On a romantic level, it looks as if one particular relationship is developing well.

TUESDAY 11th After recent trials and tribulations, beneficial Jupiter finally takes the edge off harsh influences and all manner of new beginnings are now possible. The most likely outcome of this aspect is a thorough overhaul and evaluation of your life and the introduction of much needed changes in key areas.

WEDNESDAY 12th   Mars and Jupiter are offering you opportunities to extend your range of acquaintances and broaden your field of vision. This means that you will benefit through social contacts and communications. Love, romance, glamour and parties all prove to be fortunate for you. A fruitful collaboration with a like-minded person could emerge out of today's developments and events.

THURSDAY 13th   Venus is in beautiful aspect to your ruling planet, Saturn, and this will certainly be putting a twinkle in your eye and a spring in your step. Creative projects can be completed satisfactorily now and you will feel free to turn your attention to romance, where there seems to be a good deal of action. You are certainly at your most popular.

FRIDAY 14th   The Sun is in wonderful aspect to Mercury today, influencing the property and family area of life, where there is sure to be a great deal of news. Those of you who are hoping to exchange contracts on a new home have picked an ideal time for doing so. Communications are important too, therefore ensure that you answer any telephone messages.

SATURDAY 15th   The full Moon today at the zenith of your chart advises you to think long and hard before making any professional moves. Luckily, this is the weekend and you will be unable to do so. However, it might also be a good idea for you to avoid the company of those you generally meet at work.

SUNDAY 16th   The Moon in Scorpio makes this an ideal time for visits to clubs and also for making new friends. Fresh faces will inspire you and make interesting romantic introductions. They will also help you to make up your mind over a recently acquired objective.

MONDAY 17th Today, Mercury moves into the sign of Taurus, and it is likely that you will be developing an intellectual pursuit, such as chess. Not for you the rigours of the rugby, football or baseball pitch, it is your intellect which will be getting the most exercise over the next couple of weeks. Changes to romantic situations are also likely.

TUESDAY 18th Venus is in a beautiful aspect to Neptune today, providing a rather free-wheeling and worldly attitude to the day. Certainly if you are artistic, you can put this to good use. If not, use this period for wheedling your way round a loved one who has been a little off-hand of late. New romance certainly looks promising today.

WEDNESDAY 19th Although your financial life looks more promising than it has done for some time, the Moon's position in Sagittarius today suggests that you must cast off feelings of constraint, doubt or insecurity at home. All changes should be accepted as chances to create a more stable and genial atmosphere.

THURSDAY 20th Problems of an intensely personal or emotional nature seem to have made you feel lonely, inadequate and insecure. Now, however, the influence of the Moon in your sign is about to give you back your confidence and a new purpose. Whatever your role or situation in life, this is a time to shine, blossom and succeed.

FRIDAY 21st You appear to be tempted to tackle all of life's problems independently and head-on. There are certain situations, however, that can't be solved without the help of other people. Personally, financially and professionally, everything will fit into place once you are ready to share and admit to having made a mistake.

SATURDAY 22nd Venus is in a beautiful aspect to Pluto and you can expect a certain amount of change and surprise where romantic and social matters are concerned. If you are fancy-free, this could be a time when you suddenly fall in love. You had better watch out if you are in a steady relationship. Furthermore, there is a happy glow over your friendship circle and others are happy to give you any advice that you need.

SUNDAY 23rd There seem to be two roads for you to travel. One you have tried before, so you know it leads to separation and feelings of dissatisfaction; the other can involve you in worthwhile projects and a whole new concept of romantic living, plus lasting fulfilment and enjoyment. Take the latter course and the coming weeks will be memorable.

MONDAY 24th You do, of course, have a reputation for being practical, precise and purposeful. However, you can be inflexible and conventional too, and now you must avoid restricting yourself with self-imposed limitations. In the next few weeks, success will come to you if you are ready to break certain rules and concentrate on what is original and untried.

TUESDAY 25th The recent behaviour of someone close to you seems to have caused you embarrassment or to have undermined your confidence. However, this is a time when you can begin afresh and one in which you can prove what a remarkable and forgiving individual you are by letting that other person off the hook.

WEDNESDAY 26th   This is a time for keeping a much tighter grip on the purse strings. Why let other people jeopardize what you have worked so hard to accumulate? There may be the odd emotional outburst or some ranting and raving, but you simply can't afford to throw good money after bad.

THURSDAY 27th   The Moon in Aries highlights domestic and property matters where you need to be more adventurous. A major change or upheaval is likely to take place soon. However, much will rely on the state of your relationships. Right now you may find loved ones a bit detached.

FRIDAY 28th   It is time to develop a more optimistic and positive approach to your job and career interests. You seem to be stuck in a rut at the moment, to the point where excavation is necessary, and need to find employment which allows you to prove how imaginative you really can be.

SATURDAY 29th   There will be no half measures for you today. A new Moon signifies that your personal life seems to have become confused lately, and this will be a time for changes. You are more emotional than others realize, but loyal to the end. Fantastic opportunities are beckoning today and you should not hesitate to pick up on them.

SUNDAY 30th   Mercury is in beautiful aspect to Neptune today. This is certainly good news for those of you who are creative or those who are in love. Self-expression will come naturally to you. You will be showing the more vulnerable side to your character, and loved ones will certainly be appreciative of this fact and responding to you as you would wish.

MAY

MONDAY 1st The Moon in Gemini suggests that you put the past behind you and paint on a much broader canvas. Partners and close associates may not always be compassionate or appreciative. However, new creative activities will prevent you from becoming discouraged, and you could not wish for a better time to dictate terms.

TUESDAY 2nd Mercury is lining up with your financial planet, Uranus, and it is likely that you will gain from attending meetings, negotiations or signing contracts. Certainly your ideas will be original and inspired, and if you need these characteristics for work, you will certainly be doing yourself proud.

WEDNESDAY 3rd Mercury's move into Gemini suggests that you should pay more attention to your physical wellbeing as you are likely to tire far more than usual over the next few weeks. Do not overstretch yourself or take on burdens that will weigh you down to the point where you are bent double. This is a good time for hiring the services of other people, and is particularly good if you are in the service industries.

THURSDAY 4th Venus is in a beautiful aspect to Jupiter and if ever there was a time for you to relax and enjoy yourself, this is certainly it. Creative work will be bringing in rewards, and there will be many chances for you to have fun, both today and in the future. All should be snapped up as you need time to let off steam.

FRIDAY 5th   Uranus, your financial planet, now moves into retrograde action, and you may find it difficult to make progress where money is concerned over the next few weeks. Do not fret about this, but rather lay down a new budget for you to stick to and control your spending for the time being.

SATURDAY 6th   Astrological books and magazines rarely pay very much attention to your emotional needs or responses. However, right now it is likely that you have been so concerned with personal matters that other areas of life may have been neglected. Remember that life is a process of knowing when to let go, both of conditions and individuals, in order that a new pattern can emerge. If you are an astute Capricorn you will see that there are relationships based on mutual trust to be enjoyed.

SUNDAY 7th   Practical problems appear to be stopping you from enjoying a close relationship. This is the time you will come to realize that trying to control individuals makes contentment and serenity impossible. The time has come to let go completely.

MONDAY 8th   The Moon in Leo indicates that today will be decisive for joint financial arrangements, business and legal and property matters. An awkward situation has been confronted head-on and you will be able to plan ahead with greater confidence.

TUESDAY 9th   Today the Moon in Virgo is likely to make you appreciate the many advantages to be gained by beginning to be more adventurous at home. Do, however, tread carefully concerning major professional or career matters right now, as the situation will be changing every hour.

WEDNESDAY 10th   You are likely to be feeling more in tune with your surroundings and environment, and even quite excited because the time has arrived for you to explore new areas. Even recent arguments and conflicts over money are not about to restrain you.

THURSDAY 11th   Most of us suffer from areas of confusion, disquiet and apprehension, but you appear to have allowed your fears to get out of control. Start this next few weeks with a determination to try to keep your fears at bay until you know the entire score. Ring the changes at work if you know you are being held back.

FRIDAY 12th   Mercury is beautifully aspected by expansive and benevolent Jupiter today. Therefore you are likely to be more optimistic and cheerful about the future. Should you want a time for making changes or for travelling, then this is certainly an ideal time for doing so. There seems to be plenty of news in connection with the family.

SATURDAY 13th   No one is going to give you the run-around or shout you down today. In fact, you are likely to be the person who decides how things will or won't be done. Despite this, you may find it advisable to go along with suggested changes where domestic life is concerned, and even endorse a major change or move of some description.

SUNDAY 14th   The full Moon in the area of your chart devoted to friendship and club activities suggests you tread carefully when in the company of old friends. It will not take much to offend them, as they are in a vulnerable mood and could certainly benefit from some compassion and caring on your part. Do not be found wanting.

MONDAY 15th The Moon in Sagittarius seems to suggest that you are contemplating the end of a chapter where your domestic life is concerned, and are wondering if the time is right to implement a new plan or operation. The answer to this is in the affirmative. Where work is concerned, you appear ready to take on more challenging roles.

TUESDAY 16th The Sun is in a beautiful aspect to Neptune in your sign, and this will be resurrecting the idealistic, romantic and mystical side to your personality. Should you need these characteristics where work is concerned, then you will be doing well. Romance is very well starred. Give in to feelings of romance and sentiment, and do not stifle them.

WEDNESDAY 17th There is much to be said for keeping a high profile now that the Moon is in your sign. It is also a time for keeping things simple and uncomplicated, not because the tide has turned against you, but because you no longer need to do all the organizing. What happens out of the blue will make you realize that the best results are achieved quietly without much ado.

THURSDAY 18th Venus moves into the pleasure and romance area of life. You will therefore be enjoying a month when you are at your most creative and fun-loving. Certainly if you are involved in the arts, much good work can be done. However, if you are in a steady relationship, flirtatious behaviour could get you into hot water on occasions.

FRIDAY 19th The Moon in Aquarius, the area related to money, advises you against being over-generous and making changes to long-standing financial arrangements. When out shopping, search for bargains. It doesn't matter how much money you have stashed away, you should be cautious for a while longer.

SATURDAY 20th You are certainly gifted with many talents, but they need encouragement in order to blossom. Therefore don't imagine that it is wiser to travel alone. Material and financial success will come to those who are ready to let others guide them and who understand that certain involvements are too much of a drain and must be placed on a totally different footing.

SUNDAY 21st The Sun is in beautiful aspect to Uranus and you should be attracting positive financial opportunities today. You will instinctively know which ones to reject and which ones to accept. Listen carefully while out socializing and you could be picking up financial tips. Friends may be springing a few surprises.

MONDAY 22nd Today, the Sun moves into Gemini, the area which represents the way in which you express yourself emotionally. It is also the area of service and craftsmanship. Failure to adapt may lead to a lack of progress and consequently frustration. Therefore, be aware of these pitfalls and in this way you should be able to avoid them.

TUESDAY 23rd The Moon in Pisces will certainly be keeping you on the move from morning to night, and although you may not achieve a great deal, you will certainly be stimulated by the many people you meet throughout the day. Romantically, this will be a time for brief encounters, so do not take other people too seriously.

WEDNESDAY 24th Mercury has now moved into retrograde movement and you would be ill-advised to sign any important documents or pursue legal matters over the ensuing weeks. Wait until this planet has resumed forward action.

THURSDAY 25th The Moon in Aries is highlighting domestic and property matters where it is permissible to make minor changes, but nothing major for the time being. Should you be entertaining at home this evening, you will certainly be enjoying yourself. You will be letting off steam and will be great company.

FRIDAY 26th Today, that fiery, sexy planet Mars moves into the sign of Virgo, and because of this it is likely that you could be attracted to those who come from very different backgrounds from yourself. You are also likely to be energetically chasing new goals, and wanting to make fresh changes. You will be more adventurous than you have been for some time.

SATURDAY 27th Mars lines up with Uranus today, and this period is likely to be lively. You must be ready to take advantage of the conditions around you, particularly where finances are concerned. Expect a few changes within the family circle.

SUNDAY 28th Today the Moon is in the sign of Taurus, so go ahead and enjoy yourself. Forget about your cares and worries for the time being and give yourself over to romance, socializing and sheer enjoyment.

MONDAY 29th   This is new Moon day and it is likely
to bring a fresh set of circumstances into your working
environment. Never mind, it is time to ring the changes
anyway – all you need to be is as adaptable as possible.
Listen to the words of colleagues. Amongst what they
are saying is a certain wisdom you are advised to
accept.

TUESDAY 30th   This is a day when you may run out of
steam rather more quickly than usual. Therefore stream-
line your activities during this period. An early night
would not go amiss, particularly if there is someone
special in your life, and you can share it. The telephone
is likely to be busy early this evening, but do not run
up unnecessary bills.

WEDNESDAY 31st   Today the Moon moves into the
sign of Cancer, and this will be bringing fresh circumstances to relationships, both at work and at home.
If you are fancy-free, fresh faces will seem unusually
attractive, and you could become involved with someone rather special.

JUNE

THURSDAY 1st   The Moon in Cancer today suggests
that you are really not going to feel whole without
your partner. So do go out of your way to give more
easily to those closest to you. It is certainly going to
be appreciated. In turn, they will give you the support
you want. The same advice applies in your professional
life. This is certainly a day for working in harness with
others. Life at home is likely to be delightful and it looks
as if you may have some plans for reorganizing your

environment, or perhaps you are considering taking on self-improvement activities.

FRIDAY 2nd   Today it is likely that you will need to put yourself out in order to help others, both at work and at home. Do make certain that you are keeping your stamina up by eating, relaxing and exercising sensibly, for at least some of the day. You are very rarely happy when your work is interrupted for any reason whatsoever. Therefore, be careful to be good to yourself above all else.

SATURDAY 3rd   The Moon in Leo today will help you to be outgoing and happy-go-lucky when you know you need to express yourself as fully as you possibly can. Naturally, when it comes to deep emotions, it is not as easy for you as it is for other signs, but you must make the effort. Try to make certain that you are surrounded by loved ones, children or special companions during the evening.

SUNDAY 4th   You may wake this morning wishing to retreat into a quiet corner in order to reflect or just be sentimental. Naturally, this simply will not be possible. Nevertheless, do not set yourself too pressured a schedule today, and try to avoid being around those people who grate on your nerves. You are in a mood to be harmonious and just plain lazy.

MONDAY 5th   The Sun is in beautiful aspect to Mercury today and it is likely you will really want to make the right impression on companions by appearing bright, witty and highly intelligent. You may be too close to a particular issue, or perhaps you are getting in a muddle. It is important then that you remain as objective as you can be about important matters.

TUESDAY 6th Deep down inside you know that your finances are still in rather an unstable state at the moment. Therefore you must now give yourself every opportunity to investigate what can be done to get them back on a firmer footing. If you spend money this evening, you are sure to regret it. Surely, you can have fun without breaking the bank.

WEDNESDAY 7th The Moon is in Virgo today, suggesting that one moment you will be charming, outgoing and humorous, and the next you will withdraw into yourself, perhaps allowing negative thoughts to sink into your head. You can now indulge yourself more than you have done recently, but this should be done on a positive level, and not on a negative.

THURSDAY 8th Companions and workmates seem withdrawn or pre-occupied. This is not because you are unlovable – nothing could be further from the truth. Everything will swing the other way in a couple of days, so take this opportunity to sort out some private matters of your own. It is likely that they can benefit from some of your attention.

FRIDAY 9th Basically you know that you must have the support of friends, family and colleagues, therefore you really need to go out of your way to seek them out and compliment them when you get there – this will help to smooth your path. You are likely to be socializing with a great number of new and exciting people this evening, but it is essential that you do not overspend.

SATURDAY 10th Although you are pushing hard for recognition, it seems that you are far too anxious to obtain the approval of other people for your efforts.

Certainly it always helps to charm the right people, and in order to do so you must give as much as possible, otherwise you may be passed over for a while. However, it rarely pays off to be too dependent, but this seems to be a rare mood for you.

SUNDAY 11th Venus' move into Scorpio will certainly be raising your spirits which is a blessing at the moment. You will also find that friends are willing to help you out in any way they can, and if they extend invitations you should accept. You may experience a need to escape from your everyday problems, and find a life more exciting than the one you have. However, you are far too realistic to consider this thought for very long.

MONDAY 12th The Moon in Sagittarius suggests that it is important you spend a couple of days digging deep to find the answers you need to your financial or emotional problems. The answer is there somewhere, all you have to do is locate it. It is not a time to be evasive or even timid. Life is changing too fast for you to be unaware of what is at stake.

TUESDAY 13th This is the day of the full Moon, and there may be a tendency for you to allow yourself to be dragged down by it. However, you are master of your own fate, and with your tremendous willpower, all you need to do is fight back. Do not allow yourself to be neglected, either at work or in your personal life.

WEDNESDAY 14th The Moon in your sign throws a gloriously enthusiastic influence over you. This will elevate you above the gloom and make you forget for a while that you still haven't resolved any of the financial or emotional arguments that have been damping your spirits recently. You will be putting them on the back burner for the time being.

THURSDAY 15th There seems to be more contentment behind the scenes than you have known for some while now, and your recent trials and tribulations have taught you more than you realize. It may also be that someone is on hand to give you any help, assistance or love that you need. What more could you possibly ask for?

FRIDAY 16th You are showing an unusual tendency to look at the future through rose-coloured glasses and you could well be right that everything will work out. Alternatively, it might be a good idea to give yourself a moment or two to think things through as realistically as possible before you make any important decisions.

SATURDAY 17th Mercury resumes forward action, and therefore travel matters, legal affairs, changes and paperwork can now be undertaken with confidence. Matters related to younger members of the family will also be running along a smoother track than they have been for some time. You have quite a lot to look forward to.

SUNDAY 18th Mercury is in a beautiful aspect with Venus today, and this will certainly be injecting your social life with a good deal of fun, novelty and interesting new people. Romance has a real chance of taking off, therefore if you are single it is important that you push yourself forward. Visits you make today will receive a warm welcome.

MONDAY 19th For a change you are feeling rather heady with the success you have achieved. Somehow you cannot believe that you deserve it – believe me, you do. Your reputation in the community is soaring steadily, so take care you do not go slightly over the top and become too uppity.

TUESDAY 20th There seems precious little that you do not feel confident enough to begin right now, and it really is a great boost to know that other people share your enthusiasm and your ideas, and are willing to back you. Just be certain you don't become too narrow-minded in thinking you are always right. Consider the other person's point of view.

WEDNESDAY 21st There is a slight possibility that there could be a windfall or minor bonanza coming through now with remarkable little effort on your part. In addition to these financial gains, you can expect generous gestures from those closest to you. It looks as if they are repaying a kindness from the past. Not surprisingly then, there seems to be a good deal of intimacy and warmth around you, particularly within the family.

THURSDAY 22nd The Sun moves into your opposition today and the emphasis is definitely going to be on how you can co-operate or work in harness with other people. This will be an ideal time to form professional partnerships, and on a romantic level you seem to be in great demand. Wherever possible and in all walks of life, use other people as a sounding board before reaching final decisions and taking action.

FRIDAY 23rd Someone close to you is certainly there for you if necessary. Try to be certain they are being realistic, as they could be living in 'cloud cuckoo land' at the moment. You can often be naïve in trusting people who are a touch unreliable, and this is certainly the case today. You can now tell which friends will be around for a while, and who you can trust. Proceed with caution, and this could be a good day.

SATURDAY 24th It is likely that the Moon in Taurus will help you to feel supremely self-confident and ready to take on all comers. Therefore do not hold back in any way, shape or form. Instead, be prepared to be spontaneous, creative and warm-hearted. Life has a touch more frivolity about it than you have noticed for quite some time and you should be ready to enjoy it.

SUNDAY 25th The Moon in Gemini suggests that your health could be receiving a boost if you happen to be feeling under the weather. This should be enough to buck you up, and fill you with vitality and enthusiasm. There is also a slight possibility of you over-indulging, so if you are considering dining out this evening, then do try to eat sensibly and not subject that tummy of yours to an unbelievable onslaught.

MONDAY 26th At home you can feel more expansive and a contented atmosphere begins to descend. Possibly you have made up your mind what to do during the weeks ahead, particularly to get yourself more settled and secure, and this is reflected in your happy mood. Certainly you are going to be great company to be with at the moment.

TUESDAY 27th Your ruling planet Saturn is causing you to be in sparkling form with a touch of charisma. You certainly will possess the gift of the gab and a real knack of lifting everybody else's spirits. This is not a time to be overly cautious. Say what you feel, and others will not mind if all does not happen as you say it will. But it will.

WEDNESDAY 28th The new Moon today in your opposite sign of Cancer is likely to bring a fresh set of circumstances to existing relationships, maybe even new faces in your social scene. As always with new Moons, this is a time for embracing all that is unfamiliar to you and for being more experimental.

THURSDAY 29th It is likely that your finances will receive a real boost today, though it is just as likely that you will spend as fast as it comes in. Try to resurrect that splendid Capricornian self-discipline, and you will save yourself problems and heartaches at a later date. Socially, you seem to be spoiled for choice and can afford to be a bit 'choosy'.

FRIDAY 30th Your money planet, Uranus, is lining up with Pluto and there is likely to be a change of direction where cash is concerned. However, do not worry as you are at your most shrewd at the moment, and sure to be doing the most appropriate thing at the right time. This is also a good day for meetings with those in the financial professions, so push ahead.

JULY

SATURDAY 1st Your ruling planet, Saturn, is in glorious aspect with Neptune. Usually you are down-to-earth and practical, and positively ooze common sense, but right now you are on 'cloud nine' for some reason. This is likely to be the result of developments in your romantic life. This is a good Saturday for keeping on the move, popping in on friends and finding new ways of keeping fit and enjoying yourself.

SUNDAY 2nd You are acutely aware of the need to keep yourself to yourself. Certainly, you need time to mull over private affairs and progress to date. Should you decide to mix with friends or neighbours, you will only have to give to them – and you will not get much in the way of attention, gratitude or even thanks back. It is likely that you may opt for activity in the home.

MONDAY 3rd Friends are all around and they are busy providing you with a great lift, making you feel popular, wanted and much admired. At the moment there is much to be said for trying to make up your mind about your future options, as there seem to be at least two roads you can travel in the future. It would be a good idea to discuss possibilities with friends, family and even colleagues. In this way you will get an extra insight into what would be the wisest decision.

TUESDAY 4th You seem more than usually keen to get approval and to boost your reputation, therefore you are likely to go well out of your way to make sure that you are helpful to all those around. You have a rare ability to charm at the moment and you should use it on the right people in the right places. This evening is the best possible time for being adventurous. The further you go, the more fun you will have.

WEDNESDAY 5th Venus moves into your opposite sign of Cancer and this will throw a cosy and romantic glow over love affairs. All your relationships should go through a peaceful few weeks, and if you are fancy-free, it is entirely possible you will be meeting someone special. If you have decided to become engaged or married, you have made a wise move.

THURSDAY 6th Today, your ruling planet, Saturn, goes into retrograde movement. This will delay all your progress for a short while, but instead of sitting around fuming with frustration, you could use this time for making plans for the future and implementing them at the right time.

FRIDAY 7th You seem to be rushing around at high speed, trying to make a big impression on everyone around you. But it is likely that you may be getting into a minor muddle at various points during the day because you are being overly emotional – a rare thing for you. Try to stand back and be clear about what you are doing, otherwise those closest to you will not understand. Basically the advice is to be your usual Capricorn self.

SATURDAY 8th Your money planet, Uranus, is in beautiful aspect to Pluto, therefore there could be changes in your finances. However, you need not go into a cold sweat about this as they are likely to be good and positive. You will discover that friends are only too willing to help you out should you need any advice. Nevertheless, this is not a good time for borrowing cash from friends, as in the long run this could lead to a falling out.

SUNDAY 9th You are surrounded by many charming, supportive friends and relatives, therefore do not allow the Moon in Sagittarius to persuade you to hide yourself away or to be too defensive. Like it or not, you need more emotional connection to others right now and it is important to be open and candid with them.

MONDAY 10th Mars is in scintillating aspect to Neptune and everything connected to the home and family is certainly well-starred. Problems that may have existed between yourself and members of the family will be cleared up in record time and you will feel much more relaxed in this area. This is certainly a great time if you are entertaining at home.

TUESDAY 11th Today Mercury moves into your opposite sign of Cancer. This will bring minor changes into all of your relationships, both personal and professional. People you meet will quickly become fast friends over the ensuing weeks, and if you need to introduce fresh plans or changes to those closest to you, then now is the time for action.

WEDNESDAY 12th The full Moon today occurs in your sign and because of this you are likely to feel more insecure than usual, and will prefer to keep a low profile. There are many private affairs which need your undivided attention, and other people still seem to be preoccupied. Don't feel that it is your fault. It's just the way life is for the time being, and soon you will be indulged again. Put the finishing touches to existing projects, rather than starting anything new.

THURSDAY 13th The Moon continues in your sign, and is pushing you higher in your search for recognition and progress. You want people around to be appreciative of your efforts, therefore you are giving a great deal to them. However, there is likely to be an ulterior motive. Well, let's face it, Capricorn, you can be something of an opportunist, can't you?

FRIDAY 14th You are likely to be struggling with rather intense matters now. However, you are likely to feel that despite the hard slog there is definitely a glimmer of light at the end of the tunnel. You recognize the fact that you need to let the past go and look forward to a different future. Acceptance of this means you are half way there. Be courageous and push forward.

SATURDAY 15th   You are determined to do as much as you can for those around you, but do watch that you do not strain your energy resources too far. Sustain your level of stamina by doing what you can to eat sensibly, relax and rest. Opt for peace at home rather than painting the town various shades of purple.

SUNDAY 16th   Really there is nothing more you want out of life today than to retreat into your home or family and not budge an inch. Those of you who find it necessary to work must try to find themselves a protective little niche where you can be on your own for at least part of the day. It is important right now that you steer clear of any kind of stress or strain, and this shouldn't be difficult to do. Avoid the company of demanding friends.

MONDAY 17th   A friendly aspect between Mars and Pluto suggests that changes are likely in connection with members of the family, or even your home. If you object in any way, shape or form, now is the time to speak out before it is too late. This evening you will find your friends in an energetic mood and they will attempt to persuade you to join in some kind of physical or sporty activity. If you are not in the mood, decline politely.

TUESDAY 18th   The Moon in Aries could give rise to a considerable amount of change at home. There may temporarily be some highs followed by lows. Now you must either make a complete commitment to a member of the family or lose the affection or help of someone who is likely to play an important role in your future security and happiness.

WEDNESDAY 19th A beautiful aspect between Mars and Uranus will certainly be livening up the day's activities, particularly on the financial front where you can take the initiative. You must be ready to take advantage of the lively prevailing conditions as at this time you can charm the vultures from the trees and the slimiest snakes from the grass.

THURSDAY 20th The Moon lines up with Pluto today, suggesting that this is an ideal time for discarding old habits, modes of living and outworn ideas. Avoid and resist any tendency to cling on to that which is outworn and useless in life. You cannot rejuvenate the past, even with your considerable Capricorn determination. Therefore make a plan for the future.

FRIDAY 21st Today Mars moves to the zenith of your chart and you are now in for a period of hard, but rewarding work. However, do take care that stress does not make you over-assertive with colleagues, otherwise you could be making yourself unpopular. Turn on the charm, it will serve you well.

SATURDAY 22nd The Moon in Taurus is certainly suggesting that you cast away your problems, relax and enjoy yourself this particular day. The emphasis is on romance too, and although it is changeable, it is fun and flirtatious. Those of you with creative hobbies will certainly be impressing others within your circle. The company of children is likely to be lively, but perhaps a little too much for your current frame of mind.

SUNDAY 23rd   This seems to be a Sunday of reflection, a time when you will come to believe that certain people close to you are doing their level best to inhibit your style or progress, and the time is fast nearing when you must forget about being conventional or conservative.

MONDAY 24th   To many, you are a baffling kind of individual, for you can appear to be generous and charitable, and yet at the same time still manage to save for the proverbial rainy day. Perhaps you should allow the rest of us in on your secrets. Today it appears that some kind of career change is looming over the horizon – it must be good news. Emotionally, it is simply a question of finding new, common interests with loved ones and close companions in order to bring you together.

TUESDAY 25th   You will be making it abundantly clear to those closest to you that you have your financial life very much under control, and that no one will be allowed to restrict you any more. Practically every goat has a sad or sorry story to tell at this moment, but it is more important you show how resilient you are and bounce back, rather than dwell on unhappy experiences. The Moon in the sign of Cancer suggests that other people will be doing their level best to support you and lift your spirits and it is up to you to allow them to do so.

WEDNESDAY 26th   Mercury moves into the sign of Leo, and this will provide you with a couple of weeks sorting out matters related to the law, banks, insurance and officialdom. It may sound very boring, nevertheless these sides of life do need attention, and it is the best time for you to focus in on any difficulties that exist as you have imaginative ways of solving them.

THURSDAY 27th The new Moon today, plus a beautiful aspect between Venus and Pluto, certainly make it an ideal time for making changes. Don't be afraid to throw out what has proved to be disappointing or useless and take on board the new. This applies in all areas to life. Friends will be clamouring for your company this evening, and because of your joyous mood you will be splendid company.

FRIDAY 28th The Sun is in a beautiful aspect to Mercury today, and it is an ideal time for meetings, negotiations, attending to paperwork and signing contracts. Try a new approach to an old problem, and you will find the answer staring you in the face and you will wonder why you hadn't thought of it before.

SATURDAY 29th A beautiful aspect between the Sun and Jupiter suggests you simply cannot go wrong today. You are broadening your horizons, meeting new people and are a positive joy to spend time with. Clearly then, this is a time for pushing your luck to the limit – what have you got to lose?

SUNDAY 30th Today, Venus moves into the sign of Leo, and for some time now you have been wondering whether or not to continue in a relationship. Today it is likely that you will decide that the answer is 'yes'. Because of your hesitation, you will find the other person concerned more than ready, willing and able to co-operate with you wherever they can. This is likely to be an important day for your personal life.

MONDAY 31st   Because the Moon is in Virgo, you are probably a jump ahead of anybody else at the moment. Your mind is racing ahead and you are enjoying making other people wait and wonder about your plans for the future. Do not leave it too long or you could create a yawning chasm between yourself and someone else. This would be regrettable, to say the least.

AUGUST

TUESDAY 1st   Mars is in beautiful aspect to Jupiter today and where property and family affairs are concerned, you simply cannot go wrong. Gather your confidence in your hands and be prepared to take the initiative, instead of sitting back and tending to wait and see as you usually do. You are master or mistress at the moment. You believe it, you know it, so act accordingly. Entertaining at home could be a good idea this evening.

WEDNESDAY 2nd   You have entered a crucial period where professional or partnership affairs are concerned and the time is nearing when you must say exactly what you think and feel, both logically and objectively without becoming too intense or emotional. You now have the perfect chance to reveal all the heartache and concern you have experienced over recent months.

THURSDAY 3rd   Venus, that planet of love, is lining up with Jupiter, that planet of expansion and good times. Therefore your mood will be light, there will be a spring in your step and a twinkle in your eye, and you will be very attractive, not only to workmates and clients, but also to those who are important to you on an emotional level. Bold moves are what are called for today, and you should not hesitate to push forward into life.

FRIDAY 4th Although you are now less inclined to over-react to personal setbacks or slights, loved ones and companions are sure to tax your patience to the limit right now and chastize you for not having confided in them. However, there is such a pull towards or fascination with new involvements or opportunities that you must make a firm commitment and not let anyone force you to adjust your plans in any way, shape or form.

SATURDAY 5th No matter what you may have discovered recently, you will be well advised to wait before forcing or persuading other people to clarify their views or positions. The planets today signify that you are about to be asked to choose between an established and conventional way of living and a complete change of direction that will enable you to find a greater happiness elsewhere.

SUNDAY 6th Your feelings about a partnership or other relationship can no longer be hidden. The Moon close to Pluto signifies that the time has come to put to an end recent uncertainty. You may have to alter financial arrangements, but no one must be allowed to get the better of you.

MONDAY 7th Because the Moon is in the sign of Sagittarius, this is a time for contemplation, slowing down, and listening to that small still voice inside which will ultimately help you to solve all of your problems. Hopefully, you will now come to realize that much of what was said or implied recently was designed to upset or antagonize you. You don't have to fall into that snare any longer, particularly where work is concerned.

TUESDAY 8th   Pluto has finally resumed direct movement, and therefore any problems that you may have experienced in connection with team mates or friends now begin to evaporate. It is highly likely that they have been reluctant to co-operate with you, and you have taken their behaviour to heart. Now they will reveal why they have been reticent and you will understand.

WEDNESDAY 9th   The Moon in your sign appears to be encouraging you to cast your net over a wider field and sail into uncharted waters. A great deal is certain to be swept aside during the next couple of days by circumstances over which you have little control. This will only serve to free you from repetition, boredom and discontent.

THURSDAY 10th   The full Moon in Aquarius warns you about attempting to buy the affections of other people. It simply will not work and you will only finish up with a yawning chasm in your bank account. Neither is it a time for shopping for special purchases, so keep to your budget for the time being. When it comes to entertainment this evening, opt for things which are inexpensive. The amount of money you spend will bear little relation to how much fun you will have.

FRIDAY 11th   That quicksilver planet, Mercury, moves into Virgo today and this will throw an emphasis on matters related to the law, long distance travel and foreign affairs. These will play an important part in your life and there will be some exciting news and perhaps an offer for you to consider. If not, you will certainly be getting some brainwaves during this time, and it would be a good idea to keep a pen and pad to hand, otherwise you may forget some of those ingenious schemes.

SATURDAY 12th The Moon in Pisces this weekend will certainly be keeping you on the move. It will take little to get you up and running. However, do make sure you are organized, otherwise you may waste your time as well as your money. It is likely too that you are overly concerned with a problem in connection with a brother or a sister, but soon you will discover that they have sorted themselves out without any help or advice from you. You may even resent this fact.

SUNDAY 13th Avoid setting yourself up to be challenged or provoked, even though you are heartily sick of arguments at home. There is a lot you do not know or understand and partners and close companions have a valid point when they say that career or finances are making you tense, intolerant and nervous.

MONDAY 14th Despite the fact that you are experiencing a time of quite remarkable opportunities to improve your reputation and strengthen your position at work, you still seem to be churned up emotionally. Clearly, wrangles with loved ones are the root cause of these feelings, and as much as you would prefer others to make the first move, you must take the initiative now.

TUESDAY 15th Believe it or not, the chances of progress and growth are hidden in conflicts and challenges. Therefore, nothing is beyond your talents, strength and capabilities. Uranus and Neptune in your own sign should only make you more determined than ever to find satisfactory solutions to problems of an emotional or personal nature.

WEDNESDAY 16th   Matters of a financial or professional nature must temporarily be set aside for two good reasons. Firstly, no amount of money can buy what is being offered to you; secondly, you need to realize how protected you are and will be if you continue on the course you have chosen to follow, even if you feel lonely and out of touch with loved ones at the moment.

THURSDAY 17th   Certainly the past few weeks have been physically and mentally draining, therefore much appears to fall apart at the seams and so many promises have remained unfulfilled. However, you are born under one of the most resourceful and determined signs of the zodiac and a lot of people are now going to be amazed, even shocked, by your forthright and forceful approach to domestic and property matters.

FRIDAY 18th   Now, you really must take loved ones into your confidence. Stop imagining that you alone can control half the minds and situations of the world. You may be born under one of the most industrious and tireless signs of the zodiac, but there comes a time in everyone's life when we have to lean on others, not only for practical assistance, but also for moral support.

SATURDAY 19th   Avoid packing too much into your time as the Moon suggests you could tire more easily than usual. Perhaps exertions of recent weeks are beginning to catch up with you. If this should be the case, then potter around at home, and in your own quiet way you will actually enjoy yourself.

SUNDAY 20th   Venus is in a beautiful aspect to the Sun, and because of this you cannot wait to get out into the world and enjoy yourself. That means you couldn't have a better day for letting off steam or for following your romantic interest. Those of you involved in artistic pursuits should find this a fulfilling and gratifying time.

MONDAY 21st Where work is concerned, it is a 'nose to the grindstone' period. Nevertheless, there seems to be a lot of gossip and movement in connection with colleagues and this could help you to get through the day without becoming bored. The last thing you need to do this evening is to mix business with pleasure, as you need stimulation. Go out of your way to find it.

TUESDAY 22nd The Moon is in your opposite sign of Cancer today, and this will be highlighting your relationships with those closest to you. Changes and adjustments may be necessary if you are to continue in the direction you have been pursuing, but it won't be difficult for you to find some adaptability today. If you are fancy-free, new people will be rousing your curiosity.

WEDNESDAY 23rd Today, that planet of love, Venus, will be moving into Virgo, and will be throwing a happy glow over everything connected with foreign affairs, legal matters and long distance travel. If you are fancy-free, you are sure to be drawn to those who come from different lands, and people who were reared in very different backgrounds to yourself. Never mind, variety is the spice of life.

THURSDAY 24th Today, the Sun moves into the sign of Virgo and it is likely that during the next few weeks you will develop the need to improve either your mind, your body or your image. Health regimes adopted now have a strong chance of being successful, so take them on board and be ready to work towards a new you, which everybody around will most certainly appreciate.

FRIDAY 25th   Today Mercury is in beautiful aspect to Neptune, supplying you with extra inspiration and imagination. If you need these commodities at work, then you will certainly be in for a productive and progressive day. News is likely to crop up this evening in connection with a close relative, perhaps a brother or sister.

SATURDAY 26th   The new Moon today falls in the sign of Virgo. This seems to suggest that you are learning a lesson from past experience and putting it to practical use in the present. This is also a good time for making changes in all areas of life and you are likely to meet new people who soon become fast friends. Jot down ideas as you may be able to use them in the future.

SUNDAY 27th   Mercury and Uranus are in a wonderful aspect today, and because of this good ideas will abound, although they will need a steadying influence if they are to be put to practical use. There may be a tendency for you to rush into action without considering the details and this is most uncharacteristic. Minor changes to financial arrangements can be made with confidence though, and you may be gaining in the form of a contract.

MONDAY 28th   This is a time for taking on board the new, and for being adventurous and innovative. Don't allow the stodgy side to your character to hold you back. Be prepared to take on new challenges, and dare yourself to tread where you have never trod before. The opposite sex is likely to be drawn to your new outlook on life.

TUESDAY 29th Today Mercury moves into the sign of Libra which is right at the zenith of your chart. You begin a few weeks of minor changes, possibly where career matters are concerned. Those of you who are out of work should step up your efforts during this period, as you could do yourself a lot of good.

WEDNESDAY 30th Minor changes taking place at work should not faze you. Fight for self-control, and stifle any hint of insecurity, as you will only be causing yourself unnecessary angst. Invitations to socialize coming from people at work should be accepted.

THURSDAY 31st Today the Moon moves into Scorpio, influencing friendship, acquaintances and contacts. It is quite likely that you may be developing a new ambition through such people. You will be receiving their backing and encouragement. It is also a good time for visits to clubs this evening.

SEPTEMBER

FRIDAY 1st Saturn is in a beautiful aspect to Neptune today and it looks as if your ideas will be taking constructive shape. Any mad inspirations should be seriously considered if they can benefit you in the near future. This is a particularly good day if you are scientifically inclined. Stifle any tendency to worry, as you seem to be on the right track in all areas.

SATURDAY 2nd Because the Moon has entered Sagittarius, you are likely to be in a contemplative mood. There is no harm in this as we all need periods for reflection, if only to make plans for the future and this is the time for doing just that. When it comes to problem solving, it will pay you to sniff around in the background, as you will be surprised what you can dig up.

SUNDAY 3rd Mercury is in wonderful aspect to Jupiter today, making it a great time for studying and travel. Be more adventurous than usual, and you will be glad you did, because you will be gleaning new ideas and meeting new faces. You will be excellent company this evening and it is up to you to make sure you keep in circulation. You will find a warm welcome awaiting you.

MONDAY 4th The Moon is in your sign and you should keep a high profile. Do not flinch from drawing attention to your talents. Generally speaking, you are the modest type and it will not do you any harm to blow your trumpet temporarily, otherwise people could take you for granted. This is a time for pushing ahead with all self-interest.

TUESDAY 5th This continues to be a time for keeping in the thick of the action, both in your professional and your personal life. You are more emotional than usual, and people closest to you will welcome the change in you as they will find you far more approachable than you usually are.

WEDNESDAY 6th The Moon in Aquarius could tempt you into minor extravagances. Unless you can really afford this, you need to control such a mood. Nevertheless, the day can be usefully spent in working out budgets or meeting up with people who can help you over cash matters. Do not be too proud to listen and take good advice.

THURSDAY 7th Today, Mars moves into Scorpio, the friendship area of life. It is likely that for a couple of weeks, regardless of your own sex, it will be the men in your circle who will be handing out the good advice – the question is, are you going to listen?

FRIDAY 8th The Moon in Pisces will lead to a great deal of activity over the next couple of days. However, it is a fortunate period if you are involved in sales, or if you are attempting to buy something at a bargain price. Listen carefully to news which comes in via relatives. When you consider what you have heard, you will realize that somewhere is an opportunity which you can turn around to your own advantage. There will be plenty of local activity going on this evening.

SATURDAY 9th Today is the day of the full Moon, and you must not allow this fact to pull you down. Simply remember that it is an ideal time for clearing out the mental and physical clutter in your life and preparing the ground for new thoughts and new ways of living. It is an ideal time for making plans, too.

SUNDAY 10th Venus is in a beautiful aspect to Neptune, and because of this the romantic and harmonious seem to come together to produce a happy and pleasant day. You will be acutely aware of all that is beautiful and sensuous, and you will be selective about your company when it comes to socializing this evening. You will want gentler and more refined people in your circle.

MONDAY 11th The Moon in Aries suggests that most of the activity today seems to be centred round the home. Possibly there is a special occasion or maybe somebody is in need of some special attention. If so, you will, of course, be ready to answer the call as you frequently do. Home entertaining will be particularly successful.

TUESDAY 12th   The Moon's move into Taurus will be bringing plenty of news in, should you be involved in teaching, the arts or sports. Romance will be flirtatious and fun, and should not be taken seriously during this period. If you are in a steady relationship during this period, you need to be a little careful as all actions could be misconstrued by your partner. Alternatively, they may simply be on to you.

WEDNESDAY 13th   Venus is in a wonderful aspect to Uranus today, and this is likely to bring new dynamic relationships into your life. Conditions around you today are likely to be amusing and lively and there could be some unexpected financial opportunities. Be ready to recognize and grab Lady Luck should she cross your path.

THURSDAY 14th   Venus is in a wonderful aspect to Pluto today, and it is possible that you may suddenly fall in love, or certainly be attracted strongly to other people, although there may be little chance of developing the relationship. Never mind, this is also a time which is positive in friendship and finance.

FRIDAY 15th   The Sun is in a wonderful aspect to Neptune today, providing a very subtle influence, with artistry and inspiration enhanced especially if you happen to be at all creative. There may be a sudden craze for theatre-going or visits to the cinema. You could be drawn to romantic music, literature or romantic situations. Certainly this is a time when you will be acting completely out of character, and those around may be baffled by your temporary mood. Nostalgia is also something which may be in evidence.

SATURDAY 16th Today, Venus moves to the zenith of your chart, which is certainly good for those of you who work in creative jobs or who are involved in professional partnerships. It will pay you to mix business with pleasure wherever possible over the next few weeks, particularly if you are angling for promotion or are out of work. Regardless of your own sex, females will be coming up with some good ideas, and it is up to you to listen.

SUNDAY 17th The Moon in Cancer will certainly be making those closest to you changeable over the next couple of days. Luckily they may also gladden your heart and lift your spirits. If you are fancy-free, you could be meeting someone special, therefore get out and about as much as possible.

MONDAY 18th Whilst yesterday you were able to cope with the vagaries and whims of those closest to you, today you become a little impatient. You are intent on your own progress and you will not thank others for side-tracking you. However, try to keep a civil tongue in your head, otherwise you could offend their sensitivity.

TUESDAY 19th Today the Sun and Uranus are in wonderful aspect and this is likely to produce sudden drastic changes. Guard against impulsiveness whilst being ready at least to consider financial opportunities which are being dangled in front of your eyes. Monies that are owed can be cheerfully chased and this should produce results in the near future.

WEDNESDAY 20th You will be tempted to avoid a situation connected with a legal matter or with bureaucracy. However, there is no need to panic. Providing you are open and your usual straightforward self, you will have nothing to fear. If not, you may need to do some fast talking. Get out your thinking cap.

THURSDAY 21st Today, you are able to identify with someone who seems to be going through a rather difficult phase, and are more than ready to help them out in any way you can. This is fine, just as long as you do not lend money that you can ill-afford to spend. If you do, you can certainly kiss it goodbye. You are more emotional this evening and that special someone in your life is sure to notice.

FRIDAY 22nd Today, Mercury goes into retrograde action which means the next few weeks are not the best times for long distance travelling or signing contracts. If it becomes necessary for you to do so, you will save yourself a lot of trouble by doing a great deal of double-checking. In fact, you cannot be too thorough.

SATURDAY 23rd The Moon in Virgo makes you a little dreamy today, and for some reason or other you could be recalling the past. Perhaps something occurs which seems vaguely familiar to you and takes you back several years. Those closest to you may not quite understand this mood, and you might find it difficult to explain without hurting someone's feelings.

SUNDAY 24th Today is the new Moon, a time then for sweeping away the past in readiness to step into the present and the future. Any new situation which arises, or any faces you meet which are likely to be important to you should be embraced with both arms. Should you want a time for pushing ahead with anything important, in any area to life, well then this is it.

MONDAY 25th The Sun is now firmly ensconced in the sign of Libra at the zenith of your chart, and will tend to throw the emphasis on career and work matters over the next few weeks. The trouble with you, Capricorn, is when you focus in on work matters, you tend to neglect other areas of life. If you do, you can expect to hear some loud complaints from loved ones.

TUESDAY 26th Keep a high profile at work and be prepared to make changes and adjustments should they become necessary. Colleagues seem to be clamouring for your advice and there is a great deal to boost your flagging morale and spirits. By the time you return home this evening, you should be feeling quite good and secure within yourself. Continue the day by getting out and about this evening, as your positive mood will increase your popularity.

WEDNESDAY 27th Today the Moon moves into Scorpio, the friendship, contact and acquaintances area of life. Therefore if you need any favours from these people, now is the time to leap into action. This evening you could do worse than visit a club where you will meet new people and there is a possibility of romance.

THURSDAY 28th This is a time for establishing a fresh approach to old problems. Situations have been continuing for far too long and you are anxious to see the back of them. Your imagination today will allow you to know what needs to be done at the right time, and how to eliminate an irritant from your life. Be sure you are out socializing this evening, as you are in a fun-loving mood.

FRIDAY 29th The Moon in Sagittarius temporarily pricks your bubble. You prefer to stick to routine and potter round your house deep in thought. However, do not totally block out loved ones as you may unintentionally hurt their feelings. You simply can't explain how you feel, but if they care about you, as I am sure they do, they will understand.

SATURDAY 30th Mercury and Venus are in a beautiful aspect today, and this is certainly an ideal time for getting ideas down on paper. Social life will be more than usually pleasant, and although your love life will be changeable, this will only prove to stimulate you. Those of you with a creative hobby may be finding a way of turning it to profit in the very near future.

OCTOBER

SUNDAY 1st What you need, my Capricorn friend, is a certain amount of peace and quiet today. You feel the need to escape the hubbub and traumas of the outside world but need to explain your current mood to those closest to you, otherwise they may feel neglected and shut out. When you become anti-social you do not do it by halves. You go the whole hog and this can create an unfortunate impression of isolation.

MONDAY 2nd Luckily the Moon has now entered your sign, and you are ready to get back to life in a big way. You feel instinctively that things are turning around and that you will soon be back in favour and you will be right. Spruce up your image in readiness for all of the activity that lies ahead. Romantically you could be attracting several new admirers.

TUESDAY 3rd The Moon continues in your sign, making this an ideal time for reviewing your progress to date and attempting to discover whether adjustments to plans are necessary. If so, don't hesitate to implement them now. This evening an uncharacteristically romantic mood descends and you need someone special to spend your time with.

WEDNESDAY 4th The Sun is in beautiful aspect to Jupiter, making it an excellent time for travelling. Also finances are likely to improve and this is definitely a time to push ahead with all of your plans, no matter what area of life you wish to advance. This is a good time too for those of you who need to contemplate and think about the future, as you are likely to find the answer to a long-standing problem.

THURSDAY 5th Neptune resumes forward motion, and this will throw a blanket of peace over contentious relatives. News from a brother or sister should be positive and you will receive much encouragement from this direction. Do not hesitate to confide in someone if you feel you need a sounding board before you decide in what direction you should move next.

FRIDAY 6th Now that your money planet, Uranus, has resumed direct movement, you will find over the following weeks that finances will be improving in leaps and bounds. There is no need to worry any longer, but do be ready to take on board profitable ideas which could enrich you in quite a big way. Don't allow anybody to deflect you from your purpose.

SATURDAY 7th   A beautiful aspect between Mars and Saturn produces a stop/go influence to the day and your progress is likely to be uneven. Luckily, energy and vitality are likely to be on the upsurge and you are ready to take the initiative whenever you see an opening. Sexually, the blood is coursing through your veins and the opposite sex had better watch out.

SUNDAY 8th   The full Moon today occurs in the sign of Aries and this could see off a domestic problem which has been troubling you for some time. However, if you are entertaining at home you had better double-check that guests have not been forgotten as you are likely to be more than usually absent-minded. Should you be planning a quiet day, then you should use it to clear out cluttered cupboards and useless possessions which you have been clinging on to for no good reason.

MONDAY 9th   This is an excellent day for those of you involved in home or property matters, however remotely. It is also a good time for sorting out a misunderstanding with parents or other members of the family. It is likely that you have been playing the role of disciplinarian and taking it too far. You will quickly discover today that a softer approach will pay off with other people. Should you want a time for making home improvements, then this is an ideal evening.

TUESDAY 10th   Today Venus moves into the sign of Scorpio, and because of this you will find that contacts, acquaintances and friends will be more than willing to help you out in any way they can over the next few weeks. Invitations will pour in and you will begin to feel the warmth and comfort of other people which will boost your ego and make you realize just how valuable you are.

WEDNESDAY 11th An attractive aspect between Neptune and Mars today draws you to artistic, colourful things. Furthermore, inspiration and romanticism are also emphasized and this is likely to be a happy day. When you arrive home from work this evening, you are sure to find a warm welcome. If you are fancy-free, force yourself out into the big wide world as your popularity is not in any question.

THURSDAY 12th The Moon in Taurus suggests the day may get off to a light-hearted start. However, as the hours tick away, so the planet comes into contact with Pluto and this is likely to produce a certain amount of conflict within situations and also within yourself. The best thing you can do is to remain as adaptable as possible and to avoid making any important moves in your personal life.

FRIDAY 13th There is certainly plenty of movement at work, and also loads of gossip and change within the lives of your colleagues. The day will whiz past before you know what is happening. This is an excellent time too for getting health or dental check-ups, simply to put your mind at ease.

SATURDAY 14th Finally Mercury resumes direct movement and therefore you can push ahead with matters connected with work, documents, legal matters and also with making minor changes in all areas. Problems connected with younger people are likely to evaporate as if by magic, and you begin to realize the road ahead is completely clear.

SUNDAY 15th Mars and Uranus are together today in the heavens. This then is likely to be an energetic and original day and one when you will be grasping situations extremely quickly. This time will be more than usually eventful and originality is certainly highlighted, particularly in connection with the home and finances. If you are looking for romance, then this should not be difficult as you have a certain charisma about you at the moment.

MONDAY 16th Like it or not, you will have to acquiesce to the hopes and wishes of other people today. Prepare then to play a supporting role, and do so without question or resentment. Although you prefer to be your own guiding light, this isn't possible every day of your life, a fact you need to accept.

TUESDAY 17th You are at your most restless today, due to the fact that the Moon is in your opposite sign, and because of this you must keep yourself busy to stave off negative feelings. Providing you keep your mind occupied, you will be able to retain a positive attitude to life and thereby will attract chances to you.

WEDNESDAY 18th A question of principle seems to be at stake today and you refuse to budge even an inch. The other person involved here can be equally intractable, and this could lead to bad feeling. Later on this evening, you will realize that this state of affairs cannot go on and will be more than prepared to meet the other person half way. Why don't you get on the phone and tell them so?

THURSDAY 19th Mars is in close aspect with Pluto today, giving you added force and energy. However, unless you get yourself highly organized in your usual Capricorn fashion, then life could become uneven and bottled up emotions may finally explode. Get out in the company of friends this evening, as they are likely to have a soothing effect on you.

FRIDAY 20th The Sun is in beautiful aspect with Mercury today at the zenith of your chart. You can expect a hectic time at work, although you will find the increased activity stimulating. There will be plenty of discussions going on at a professional level and the outcome should work to your benefit. Your stimulation is likely to spill over into your private life this evening and you will want to share all with that special someone in your life.

SATURDAY 21st Today Mars moves into the sign of Sagittarius, and you will now have the happy knack of turning everything to your advantage. However, you may be strongly impulsive and should stop in your tracks before making important moves, just in case you are going off into the blue yonder without sufficient facts tucked underneath your belt. If you are in a steady relationship, there will be occasions when you will be strongly tempted to stray. This needs conscious controlling.

SUNDAY 22nd The Moon in Virgo suggests that the further you get away from your usual haunts and places, the more stimulated you will be. See what you can do to persuade loved ones to try fresh interests and experiment with new hobbies. Without plenty to do today, you could become bad-tempered, although this is easy to avoid if you take this advice.

MONDAY 23rd The Moon at the zenith of your chart suggests you keep as high a profile as possible where professional matters are concerned so you attract good fortune to you. Neither should you shrink from airing your views or presenting your creative ideas as they could go a long way to helping you fulfil your ambition. You may not have a great deal of energy left in the evening and a quiet time is recommended.

TUESDAY 24th Today is the day of the new Moon, and it falls in the sign of Scorpio. This seems to suggest you will be meeting new faces, both on a professional and personal level, and if you are single this could very well lead to romance. If not, it may be that you are trying to get one of your ideas off the ground and you should be successful. This evening, you will find loved ones in an energetic and passionate mood.

WEDNESDAY 25th Mercury lines up with Jupiter today, making it an excellent time for dealing with matters connected with travel and foreign countries. Finances could be improved too and it is time to push ahead with your plans. Your imagination is at its most colourful, and if you need this in your work, you will certainly be putting in a good account for yourself. Your mood will be so buoyant that you will rise above any petty arguments amongst colleagues and you will be likely to gain their respect.

THURSDAY 26th For the sake of your long-term financial security, you must be ready to reconsider decisions and perhaps adopt a different attitude. It might also be a good idea to agree that you are partly to blame for a disturbing state of affairs because you misinterpreted a situation. Alternatively, you may have tried to keep people on too short a rein.

FRIDAY 27th Communication and travel plans are prominent now. However, much relies on the outcome of an intensely personal dispute. Do everything within your power to reach an early friendly settlement, even if it means eating humble pie, because, after all, it is your future happiness which really counts.

SATURDAY 28th Unless you do things by the book or accept established codes of behaviour, you could be caught napping over important career moves. The stars today signify that you must fulfil every promise to the letter and prove how discreet and reliable you can be.

SUNDAY 29th You are now given the chance to break the pattern of a lifetime and prove just how ready you are to find fame and fortune in a completely different direction. You have deliberated for some time. Now you must get to work and make a number of decisive moves.

MONDAY 30th Do let others know that they are doing you a favour by bringing everything out into the open. Changes at home and at work have been discussed for quite some time, but you haven't had the courage to face them until now. Now you have, and life looks considerably brighter.

TUESDAY 31st Venus is in a beautiful aspect to Uranus today, and because of this, new dynamic relationships can occur. Financial opportunities are also likely and you must be ready to grab all chances that come your way. Certainly right now life is quite amusing and lively. Money spent on entertainment this evening will not be going to waste.

NOVEMBER

WEDNESDAY 1st The month begins on a dramatic note due to a fantastic aspect between the Sun and Pluto. This is likely to bring turbulent changes into your life, as well as a new outlook. There could be a certain amount of upheaval, not without strain. However, all efforts made now will be rewarded in the near future, although you may need to discard old patterns of behaviour as well as ideas which may be close to your heart.

THURSDAY 2nd   Venus is in beautiful aspect to Pluto today, and this will certainly be increasing your chances of extracting favours from contacts, friends and loved ones. Few can deny you at the moment, and it is especially lucky for you if you work as a member of a team or a professional partnership. Emotionally, you may feel that progress is unlikely, and your intuitions will prove correct.

FRIDAY 3rd   Today, Venus moves into Sagittarius and you need to be a little careful over the ensuing weeks as there is the distinct possibility that you could become involved with a married person who could be harmful to you. A little bit of time spent investigating will pay off and save you a great deal of heartache. Nevertheless if you work in research or behind the scenes, you are certainly in for a productive few weeks.

SATURDAY 4th   Today, Mercury moves into the friendship area of your life and it is likely that fresh faces will be entering the scene and will find a warm welcome waiting for them. There seems to be a certain amount of change and gossip in your intimate circle, and you must be careful not to hand on secrets that you have sworn to keep to yourself, otherwise your popularity could plummet.

SUNDAY 5th   The Moon is in Aries this Sunday, and because of this you will be inclined to stay close to home rather than being adventurous. Nevertheless, people will be popping in and you will find their company stimulating. You seem to be turning over decisions in your mind, but you will not arrive at any satisfactory conclusion for the time being.

MONDAY 6th The Moon in Taurus will certainly be throwing a lively glow over your life and your popularity will be soaring. In fact, you will find you are hard put to fulfil all the social obligations you are taking on board.

TUESDAY 7th Life really seems to be a series of payments, and right now it is not the time to force the pace personally or professionally. However, this is certainly a great time for making a number of long-term plans, and also for considering all major changes that you will be able to implement in the very near future.

WEDNESDAY 8th Your personal life seems to be in a state of flux, and you must guard against appearing to be so engrossed in new ideas and plans that you upset those who are closest to you. However, planetary influence does appear to indicate that a move or change within the home must take place fairly soon.

THURSDAY 9th An unusual amount of planetary activity right now is urging you to stop running away and face up to important developments and situations which have occurred during the last couple of weeks. Above all else, become whatever you want to be, it is no use trying to force yourself into a mould which is quite alien to your normal character.

FRIDAY 10th Today you would be advised to get together with friends, as you will find them entertaining and full of gossip. You are in a very generous mood for helping others and you will find they will instinctively be coming to you for advice. A visit to a club this evening will do as well as anything for entertainment.

SATURDAY 11th Pluto finally escapes Scorpio's grips and is now entrenched in Sagittarius where it will stay for approximately nine years. During this period much of the problems that plague us at the moment, in terms of health, politics and wars, will cease to exist, and we will all have a good deal more to look forward to. You in particular, Capricorn, should be looking to the far distant future as this is the place you tend to live in. Because of this you should be filled with optimism.

SUNDAY 12th The moment has finally come for you to make certain decisive moves where your career is concerned. The stars seem to signify that you have everything to gain by taking on board the different and new. This will ensure you a greater degree of freedom and flexibility – something you secretly desire.

MONDAY 13th Recently you have shown a great deal of determination and courage and there must have been times when it was felt it would have been wiser to allow others to have their own way. However, now is not the time to flinch and you should take control of the situation. If you know you could be happier or more secure in a different setting, then it could be time to move on.

TUESDAY 14th Having recently refused to be drawn into heated debate or to give in under stress, you deserve all that is good for the next few weeks, and you are sure to receive it. It looks as if the sky is the limit in all areas. Domestic upheaval is more than a distinct possibility, and what takes place during the remainder of the month should have you planning and organizing things with new-found determination and optimism.

WEDNESDAY 15th Mercury is in a beautiful aspect to Saturn today. This suggests that you are experiencing a constructive phase as your powers of concentration are increased. Therefore if you need to attend to anything that is mentally demanding, you will be at your most efficient and will impress everybody around, including the family. Any minor changes you wish to make in your personal life will be acceptable to all.

THURSDAY 16th Mars is in wonderful aspect to Jupiter, providing you with a positive and energetic day. This is definitely a time for taking advantage of the lively prevailing conditions, and if you fail to do so you will certainly live to regret it. It is also a good time for sorting out confusion, muddle and disagreement between relatives. Many of you will experience a desire to improve your surroundings.

FRIDAY 17th It is time to be bolder, to paint on a larger canvas, to experiment with life and generally to be more daring. Naturally, this means stepping out of your Capricorn mould, but you will delight in adopting a new image and observing the startled faces on those who thought they knew you well.

SATURDAY 18th This may be a weekend, but your thoughts are very much preoccupied with work and ambition. This is so much so that loved ones could feel they are being neglected and they will not hesitate to say so. Divide up your time equally between your private thoughts and your social life.

SUNDAY 19th It seems the lure of work has proved to be too strong for you and you are in touch with colleagues. Why not mix business with pleasure? In this way you will be able include that very special someone in your life. It is unlikely they will mind you discussing business for a little while, but do not do so for the entire evening.

MONDAY 20th Finally, your ruling planet Saturn resumes direct movement and your progress from now on will be nothing short of startling. Instead of experiencing the distinct impression that for every step you take forward it is necessary to retrace six paces, you can now push ahead unimpeded by loved ones or obstacles in any guise. The road ahead is clear, Capricorn, so go after your dreams and make them materialize.

TUESDAY 21st A beautiful aspect between Venus and Mars will certainly be creating harmony at work, in your friendship circle and at home. Where career matters are concerned, you are prepared to take the initiative and responsibility for your actions and others will be admiring your courage. On a personal level, you seem to be earning appreciation and love from the family, and the whole day provides you with a great deal to look forward to.

WEDNESDAY 22nd This is the day of the new Moon and it occurs in the sign of Scorpio. This suggests that your friendship circle will be broadening quite considerably, and you are likely to be attracted to those who are totally different from yourself. Possibly you are going through one of your moods of re-educating yourself, and you need the experience of other people in order to help you to do so. Any invitations that come in should be accepted, especially if they are for tonight or tomorrow.

THURSDAY 23rd Today the Sun moves into the sign of Sagittarius, and you begin a rather contemplative few weeks. It is likely that so many moves and changes have left you breathless and you need a time for recuperation. If so, this is it and you should use it well. However, do not laze around too much. Certainly a couple of days is permissible, but after this you could become rather tetchy.

FRIDAY 24th Mercury joins the Sun in Sagittarius, and again this will encourage you to withdraw from the world. Maybe you have ideas you want to get down on paper, or perhaps you want to discuss changes that you have in mind with the family. If so, this is an ideal time to choose as you will not be distracted by outside events.

SATURDAY 25th The Moon in your sign suggests that you will be joining the human race once more. Revitalized and refreshed, you will be making a big impression on everybody around, particularly in your friendship circle. This could be a memorable weekend for romance.

SUNDAY 26th The softer side to your nature is very much in evidence and this will draw other people to you, particularly the opposite sex. Avoid making any kind of commitment as your emotions are in a state of flux, and it would be difficult to withdraw a promise or commitment at a later date.

MONDAY 27th The Moon today is in Aquarius, the area of your chart devoted to finances where a state of flux seems to exist. Try to stem the flow of your outlay and conserve as much as possible. This is a good time for financial meetings as officials are likely to be in a co-operative mood.

TUESDAY 28th Venus moves into your sign, and it will certainly show. You become more physically attractive and mentally alert and creative. If you are fancy-free, there is a strong possibility of your meeting someone new in the future. If not, it may be that you are thinking of forming a professional partnership, and this will be lucky for you.

WEDNESDAY 29th The Moon in Pisces makes it difficult for you to relax over the next couple of days and you will be finding the slightest excuse for keeping on the move. Naturally then, it would not be a good idea to commit yourself to any work which requires an eye for detail or intense concentration, as shoddy workmanship could be the result.

THURSDAY 30th You continue to dash hither and thither in a state of excitement. Maybe you have some news which you wish to impart to all and sundry. If so, you will be receiving a warm welcome. On a romantic level, it is a period of brief encounters, therefore it is essential that you do not take yourself or other people too seriously. Nevertheless, this is an enjoyable time.

DECEMBER

FRIDAY 1st Four planets zooming through your chart, including aggressive and sexy Mars, make the scene set for new developments in all areas. Past experience will be very relevant to what takes place in the near future, but the chances of your receiving a favourable response are brighter because your faith and optimism in yourself and your future are hard to resist. There is much fun going on externally, but it will be important for you to remember to give time to your home and family.

SATURDAY 2nd It looks as if a great sorting out and reorganization process is going on in your life right now and you may be surprised to discover that certain people unbeknown to you have been quietly changing their attitudes and minds as well as their plans. This is likely to affect your domestic life, and it might be a good idea to give this area your full attention so that you may update yourself on what is happening. No need to worry too much, as you are the top priority in the lives of those that mean the most to you.

SUNDAY 3rd Nothing important ever really happens until the time is right. Now the cosmic influences are suggesting that something good is about to occur. This may come as a result of a meeting, a phone call, or even a letter. The Moon in Taurus further suggests that changes are taking place on the financial front and you may have to make rapid adjustments which will come as second nature to you right now.

MONDAY 4th It looks as if events are building up for a massive reshuffle or major change, and it is important that you do not lose sight of what you really want. The more confidently you protect yourself now, the more certain is your success. Remember that Mars is giving you the courage of your convictions and you must carry these with you throughout the day ahead. Push aside doubts or insecurities, as you have a great deal going for you.

TUESDAY 5th Temporarily today it would appear that at least in one direction it seems to be a case of 'two steps forward, one back'. This may result in feelings of frustration. However, it is important that you don't weaken, because you will come out at the end in a stronger position than seems possible to you at the moment. Curb unnecessary expenses; your friends and loved ones may be trying to part you from your hard-earned cash, and you will need it in the near future.

WEDNESDAY 6th True success generally stems from the ability to know instinctively when to take action and when to hold back. This is further helped by an inclination to act on hunches, which is exactly what you should be doing at the moment. The Moon in Gemini is certainly shaking you up intellectually, and once the dust has settled you will be looking at a situation through fresh eyes and will wonder why you have been fretting about it for so long.

THURSDAY 7th The full Moon in Gemini warns you about changing your mind over one particularly major issue. If you do, you could live to regret it. Therefore keep to the master plan which you made some time ago and which to date is proving to be so successful. Should you be taking short trips today, then it would be wise to allow longer to get to your destination as there could be some hold-ups. Continue to look towards the fulfilment of your ambition with a positive attitude.

FRIDAY 8th Mercury and Jupiter are in beautiful aspect today, and you couldn't have a better time for attending to legal matters, travel or education. A spot of self-improvement wouldn't go amiss either, and would be sure to be applauded by all of those that mean the most to you. Keep in the spotlight today as this is the way to draw opportunities to you.

SATURDAY 9th You may decide that it is time to ease your way out of one part of your life. If so, you will discover that a door you have been waiting to pass through for a very long time is gradually opening. Should you feel that you can benefit from the advice or objective viewpoint of somebody else, then do not hesitate to ask for their opinion. They will be only too glad to help you out. New relationships made today are likely to be important for some time to come.

SUNDAY 10th The Sun continues to sparkle in your own sign, confirming that the best time for making new beginnings has finally arrived. You may also realize that you made a false start a couple of months ago, and are now prepared to admit it. Having done so, you will be clearing the path for greater progress. Be sure that you get out this evening in the company of other people. Somebody's sense of humour will help you to relax.

MONDAY 11th That planet of love and creativity, Venus, is in aspect with your own ruling planet, Saturn. This suggests that where anything important is concerned, you would be advised to adopt a more courteous approach. You are in a sociable mood too, and you should mix business with pleasure whenever the opportunity arises. Romantically, you are at your most attractive and are likely to be in the happy position of being able to pick and choose.

TUESDAY 12th Mercury moves into your sign, as if it is not crowded enough. This will be making it a good deal easier for you to concentrate on intricate work, and also to make the necessary adjustments to turn one of your plans into reality. Those of you signing important documents over the next couple of weeks are sure to be lucky. Don't ignore communications.

WEDNESDAY 13th Money needs expert handling if you are to enjoy what's on offer socially whilst balancing your accounts. It will pay for you to make financial allowances for the unexpected until the end of this month. Only when the expense of this time of year is over and done with will you be able to assess the cash situation and decide exactly where you go from there.

THURSDAY 14th At last your progress seems to be obvious even to you, and you finally realize that you are getting somewhere, which in turn is providing you with a much more confident and optimistic attitude. It is highly likely that you have been wondering why you didn't follow one particular line of action from the start. Never mind, it does not help to dwell on the past unless you can learn from it. Now is the time for focusing your attention on the future.

FRIDAY 15th As the pace of your life is inclined to speed up right now, it would be disastrous to follow any course of action for the wrong reason. Not only would you suffer the consequences of doing so for a long time, but you could also lose credibility. Therefore you need to dig deep inside yourself in order to check out your true motives. Unless they are really valid, then put them to one side.

SATURDAY 16th That romantic and sociable planet, Venus, is in close aspect with artistic and inspired Neptune. This is likely to make for a harmonious and loving day, as well as providing you with the chance to become involved with the financial affairs of other people. This could benefit you in the long run, provided you do your home work. This evening has a romantic feel about it.

SUNDAY 17th At present half of the planets are passing through your sign. This is an indication that good things are going to be happening to you. However, only you can choose what to take and what to leave. Providing you proceed in your usual cautious and calm way, you will sift through your many opportunities and make some wise decisions.

MONDAY 18th The Moon in Scorpio will enable you to prove to business associates and partners that you can't be defeated by setbacks or even personal rebuffs. As a goat, you are invariably industrious and constructive, as well as canny and emotional – at least underneath.

TUESDAY 19th The Sun is in wonderful aspect with beneficial and lucky Jupiter. This would be an ideal time for dealing with matters abroad or with the family. Cash matters are likely to improve and it is time to push ahead with plans. However, if you are out taking part in any last minute Christmas shopping, don't let a buoyant mood lead you into extravagance. This evening is an ideal time for pushing ahead with romance.

WEDNESDAY 20th Romantic Venus pairs up with dynamic Uranus today and this is likely to bring new relationships and attractions to your life. Life is certainly going to be amusing and lively. There may be unexpected gains or presents, and if you are combining business with pleasure, do control your flirtatious mood as it could get you into trouble with that special person in your life.

THURSDAY 21st You are looking forward to a time of greater security and stability. A position or the recognition that has been denied you in the past is sure to be yours for the asking. On a more personal level, you will no longer feel a victim of fate or circumstances. All you have to do is summon up the courage to take the first daring steps into the great unknown.

FRIDAY 22nd Today is the day of the new Moon and it occurs in the sign of Sagittarius. This will be sharpening your intuitions and it is important that just for once you ignore your practical head and listen to your instincts. Providing you can bring yourself to act on your hunches, this can be a productive and lucky period. Also, today the Sun enters your sign and you are flooded with solar power. Confidence is clearly on the upsurge.

SATURDAY 23rd Romantic and artistic Venus moves into the financial area of life which will not only account for the extra gifts you will be receiving over the next few days, but will also be bringing you opportunities to use your money wisely. It is likely you will be doing a good deal of clever bargaining in the next three to four weeks.

SUNDAY 24th Mercury and Mars today will give you additional mental energy, although impulsiveness in speech and movement could make you over-assertive. Despite this, you are feeling positive and optimistic about the future, as well as enjoying the present to its fullest extent. You will have added vitality and will be able to cope with any extra work which may be needed at home.

MONDAY 25th Certainly you will be enjoying your day and the lines of communication between yourself and your family are wide open. This is all well and good, provided you keep your conversation at a positive level and do not recriminate over past differences. This is no time for bad feelings.

TUESDAY 26th The Moon in Pisces today will at some point incline you to get out and about. Even if it is only for an hour or so, it will blow the cobwebs away. Certainly, if you are in the company of friends in high spirits, your day will be warm and welcoming. This is the right time for really relaxing and temporarily forgetting about problems and careers.

WEDNESDAY 27th You must go to some pains to ensure that partners do not feel neglected. You are provided with an opportunity to prove you are not as secretive and as self-sufficient as other people imagine. This is the ideal time, Capricorn, to show that you have a soft sentimental centre, so grab it with both hands.

THURSDAY 28th Today there is a beautiful aspect between Mercury and Neptune. This gives a refining influence, and may possibly also lead to a sudden liking for peace and quiet. Possibly the activities of recent days have caught up with you, or maybe you have overcrowded your social programme. In any event, ensure that you spend at least an hour or so on your own gathering your thoughts and really relaxing. Many of you will be hearing from somebody abroad.

FRIDAY 29th The Moon in Aries throws an emphasis on the domestic area of life where there seems to be quite a lot of activity going on. The chances are that neighbours and friends are finding that time is hanging heavily on their hands and will be popping around in order to catch up with all of the latest gossip and trying to discover how you are. Be sure that they find a warm welcome waiting for them.

SATURDAY 30th   Mars is in a wonderful aspect to Neptune today and will make you aware of all that is colourful and delicate in life. If you have artistic ability, and are not lacking in practical qualities, which would be unusual, you will get a great deal from this very lively day. Should you be fancy-free, this is a great time for taking a relationship a step further. You are feeling optimistic about the future, and looking forward to something special tomorrow.

SUNDAY 31st   Mercury is in wonderful aspect with Uranus today, and because of this originality and intellectual brightness will be evident though there might be some slight strain here. Exercise control, and prepare for some unusual eccentricities on the part of other people. Fresh faces and interesting people are likely to have a strong influence on the day, but you must ensure that they are worthwhile. Guard against becoming involved with cranks. Money spent on enjoyment today will certainly not be going to waste.

HAPPY NEW YEAR

Moon Tables

THE MOON AND YOUR MOODS

Our moods and, indeed, the strength of our intuition
are clearly affected by the Moon. After all, you may ask
yourself on occasions, why on earth does such a well-
balanced person as me suddenly become bad-tempered,
frigid, emotional or sentimental on certain days? Well,
I'm afraid it is all down to the position of the Moon.
Why not try an experiment, and attempt to prove it to
yourself?

Glance at the Moon table for any given week or month
and then put it away. In the meantime, in your diary
make notes of your moods and reactions to situations.
Once this period has expired, rescue your book, turn
to the Moon tables and you will notice a clear pattern
of behaviour developing. You don't need an astrologer
to work out for you that, during the week, or during
the period whilst you were taking notes, the Moon
was, for example, in Scorpio when you were feeling
depressed, in Cancer, maybe, when you were feeling
romantic and Aries when you developed headaches and
were bad-tempered, etc.

Your own individual pattern is likely to be repeated
monthly. However, do not give in or be surprised if you
are unaffected when the Moon passes through certain
signs. It may be, for example, that whilst it made its
way through Aries and Libra, you were neither elated

nor depressed. What does this mean? Well, such a happening would merely suggest that these two signs are not particularly prominent on your own individual birthchart.

Female readers will probably like to take note of the fact that very often their menstrual cycle, if of normal length, will begin when the Moon is in the same one or two signs, each month. Why not be a devil and experiment? Give it a try. You have nothing to lose and you may find out an awful lot about yourself.

FULL AND NEW MOONS FOR 1995

January	1st New in ♑	16th Full in ♋	30th New in ♒
February	15th Full in ♌		
March	1st New in ♓	17th Full in ♍	31st New in ♈
April	15th Full in ♎	29th New in ♉	
May	14th Full in ♏	29th New in ♊	
June	13th Full in ♐	28th New in ♋	
July	12th Full in ♑	27th New in ♌	
August	10th Full in ♒	26th New in ♍	
September	9th Full in ♓	24th New in ♏	
October	8th Full in ♈	24th New in ♏	
November	7th Full in ♉	22nd New in ♏	
December	7th Full in ♊	22nd New in ♐	

KEY

♈ Aries	♌ Leo	♐ Sagittarius
♉ Taurus	♍ Virgo	♑ Capricorn
♊ Gemini	♎ Libra	♒ Aquarius
♋ Cancer	♏ Scorpio	♓ Pisces

FULL AND NEW MOONS FOR 1995

Jan	Feb	Mar	Apr	May	Jun	Jul	Aug	Sept	Oct	Nov	Dec	
♑	♓	♓	♈	♊	♋	♌	♎	♏	♑	♒	♈	1
♑	♓	♓	♉	♊	♋	♍	♎	♐	♑	♓	♈	2
♒	♓	♈	♉	♊	♌	♍	♏	♐	♒	♓	♉	3
♒	♈	♈	♊	♋	♌	♍	♏	♑	♒	♈	♉	4
♓	♈	♉	♊	♋	♍	♎	♐	♑	♓	♈	♉	5
♓	♉	♉	♊	♋	♍	♎	♐	♎	♓	♉	♊	6
♈	♉	♉	♋	♌	♍	♏	♐	♎	♓	♉	♊	7
♈	♉	♊	♋	♌	♎	♏	♑	♓	♈	♉	♋	8
♈	♊	♊	♌	♍	♎	♐	♑	♓	♈	♊	♋	9
♉	♊	♋	♌	♍	♏	♐	♒	♈	♉	♊	♋	10
♉	♋	♋	♌	♎	♏	♑	♒	♈	♉	♋	♌	11
♊	♋	♋	♍	♎	♐	♑	♓	♉	♊	♋	♌	12
♊	♌	♌	♍	♏	♐	♒	♓	♉	♊	♋	♍	13
♊	♌	♌	♎	♏	♑	♒	♈	♉	♊	♌	♍	14
♋	♌	♍	♎	♐	♑	♓	♈	♊	♋	♌	♍	15
♋	♍	♍	♏	♐	♒	♓	♉	♊	♋	♍	♎	16
♌	♍	♎	♏	♑	♒	♈	♉	♋	♌	♍	♎	17
♌	♎	♎	♐	♑	♓	♈	♉	♋	♌	♎	♏	18
♍	♎	♏	♐	♒	♓	♈	♊	♋	♌	♎	♏	19
♍	♏	♏	♑	♒	♈	♉	♊	♌	♍	♎	♐	20
♍	♏	♏	♑	♓	♈	♉	♋	♌	♍	♏	♐	21
♎	♐	♐	♒	♓	♉	♊	♋	♍	♎	♏	♑	22
♎	♐	♐	♒	♓	♉	♊	♋	♍	♎	♐	♑	23
♏	♑	♑	♓	♈	♉	♊	♌	♍	♏	♐	♒	24
♏	♑	♑	♓	♈	♊	♋	♌	♎	♏	♑	♒	25
♐	♑	♒	♓	♉	♊	♋	♍	♎	♐	♑	♓	26
♐	♒	♒	♈	♉	♊	♌	♍	♏	♐	♒	♓	27
♑	♒	♓	♈	♉	♋	♌	♎	♏	♑	♒	♈	28
♑		♓	♉	♊	♋	♌	♎	♐	♑	♓	♈	29
♒		♈	♉	♊	♌	♍	♎	♐	♒	♓	♈	30
♒		♈		♋		♍	♏		♒		♉	31